STARK

SprachenZertifikat Englisch A2

Common European Framework A2

Übungsaufgaben im Stil der Prüfung

mit Audio-CD

STARK

Bildnachweis

Umschlag (von li nach re):
© Gary718/Dreamstime.com; © Can Balcioglu/Dreamstime.com; © Jack Rogers/Dreamstime.com
Seite 5: © Willselarep, Image provided by Dreamstime.com
Seite 10: © Claudiodivizia/Dreamstime.com
Seite 11: © John Quinn/Dreamstime.com
Seite 16/17: © Claudia Bauer
Seite 21: © Phaif/Dreamstime.com
Seite 22: © Kongxinzhu/Dreamstime.com
Seite 38: www.asap.co.uk
Seite 39: © Mark Huls/Dreamstime.com
Seite 44 (von li oben nach re unten):
© Simon Krzic/Dreamstime.com; © Dana Johnson/Dreamstime.com;
© Andrey Armyagov/Dreamstime.com; © Thorntons UK
Seite 45 (von li oben nach re unten):
© Nikolay Okhitin/Dreamstime.com; © Carl Keyes/Dreamstime.com;
© Ernst Daniel Scheffler/Dreamstime.com; © Robwilson39/Dreamstime.com;
© Nikolaev/Dreamstime.com; © Oli Mohd/www.sxc.hu; © Olivier Tuffé/fotolia.com;
© David Hughes/Dreamstime.com; © Purmar/Dreamstime.com
Seite 49: © Hareluya/Dreamstime.com
Seite 50: © Cyclope/Dreamstime.com
Seite 66: "Lady Godiva"' by John Collier (died 1934)
Seite 67: © Ben Goode/Dreamstime.com
Seite 72 (von li oben nach re unten):
© Yordan Mihaylov/Dreamstime.com; © Olga Utlyakova/Dreamstime.com;
© Palabra/Dreamstime.com
Seite 73: © Rafael Ramirez Lee/Dreamstime.com; © Sebastian Czapnik/Dreamstime.com;
© Sugarfree.sk/Dreamstime.com; © Igor Terekhov/Dreamstime.com; © Claudia Bauer
Seite 77: © Shariff Che' Lah/Dreamstime.com
Seite 78: © Andreas Resch/Dreamstime.com
Seite 94: http://en.wikipedia.org/wiki/File:Hotdogamsterdam.JPG
Seite 95: http://en.wikipedia.org/wiki/File:Ocarina_SopranoF_AltoC.jpg
Seite 100 (von re oben nach li unten):
© Robert Pernell/Dreamstime.com; © Ximagination/Dreamstime.com;
© Michael Komm/Dreamstime.com
Seite 101: © Jason Stitt/Dreamstime.com; © Stickyredhead/Dreamstime.com; http://en.wikipedia.org/wiki/File:2009_0123sokminden_0317.JPG; © Bonfils Fabien/Dreamstime.com;
© Martin Dimitrov/Dreamstime.com; © Tdoes1/Dreamstime.com;
© Saksoni/Dreamstime.com; http://en.wikipedia.org/wiki/File:Blyskawica_I_d.jpg; http://en.wikipedia.org/wiki/File:Windsor_Castle_at_Sunset_-_Nov_2006.jpg;
Seite 105: © Tal Kalimi/Dreamstime.com
Seite 106: © Elena Elisseeva/Dreamstime.com
Seite 122: http://en.wikipedia.org/wiki/File:Reuterdahl_-_Sinking_of_the_Titanic.jpg
Seite 123: http://en.wikipedia.org/wiki/File:London_Eye_-_TQ04_26.jpg
Seite 128 (von li oben nach re unten):
© Olga Nayashkova/Dreamstime.com; © Vinicius Tupinamba/Dreamstime.com;
© Joe Gough/Dreamstime.com; © Jelenaprastalo/Dreamstime.com;
© Karen Struthers/Dreamstime.com; © Bidouze Stéphane/Dreamstime.com
Seite 129 (von li oben nach re unten):
© Jacus/Dreamstime.com; http://en.wikipedia.org/wiki/File:Bianchi.JPG;
© Sergey Berezin/Dreamstime.com; © Pavel Losevsky/Dreamstime.com;
© Sergeymakarenko/Dreamstime.com; © Andres Rodriguez/Dreamstime.com;
© Spe/Dreamstime.com (Muffins); © Danny Smythe/Dreamstime.com (Bread);
© Suzanne Tucker/Dreamstime.com (Milk)
Seite 133: © Maigi/Dreamstime.com
Seite 134: © Irochka/Dreamstime.com

ISBN 978-3-86668-113-2

www.stark-verlag.de
1.Auflage 2009

Inhalt

Autorin:
Michaela Kamm

Vorwort

Liebe Schülerin, lieber Schüler,

der Erwerb eines international anerkannten Sprachenzertifikats gewinnt immer mehr an Bedeutung. Die Prüfungsanforderungen sind standardisiert und somit werden Leistungen und Kenntnisse länderübergreifend vergleichbar. Die erfolgreiche Teilnahme gilt somit als europaweiter Sprachkompetenznachweis, da sich die Zuordnung der Sprachenzertifikate am Gemeinsamen Europäischen Referenzrahmen (GER) orientiert. Speziell als Ergänzung zu einem Schulabschluss oder um sich bei einer Bewerbung für einen Praktikums-, Ausbildungs- oder Arbeitsplatz von den anderen Kandidaten abzuheben, lohnt sich der Einsatz auf jeden Fall. Mit einem Zertifikat weisen Sie nach, dass Sie in allen vier Kompetenzbereichen *(Reading, Writing, Listening und Speaking)* über im (Arbeits-)Alltag einsetzbare Kenntnisse verfügen.

Die folgenden Tipps und Hinweise sowie die zusammengestellten *Mock Exams* sollen Ihnen helfen, Ihre Prüfung für das Sprachenzertifikat A 2 erfolgreich zu meistern.

Wie sieht der Test aus?

Der Test gliedert sich meist in vier Teile, wobei *Reading* und *Writing* zusammengefasst sein können. Im *Reading*-Teil werden (überwiegend im *multiple choice*-Format) Vokabel- und Grammatikkenntnisse sowie das Textverständnis abgeprüft. Eine offenere Frage ist die *Writing*-Aufgabe, bei der Sie eine kurze Mitteilung, ein E-mail oder einen Brief nach vorgegebenen Stichpunkten verfassen müssen.
Bitte denken Sie unbedingt daran, dass Sie alle Antworten noch auf den Antwortbogen übertragen müssen. Bei manchen Prüfungsanbietern steht Ihnen dafür keine zusätzliche Zeit mehr zur Verfügung.

Im *Listening*-Teil haben Sie, je nach Prüfungsanbieter, einige Minuten Zeit, um Ihre Antworten aus dem Aufgabenheft auf den Antwortbogen zu übertragen. Deshalb arbeiten Sie solange die CD läuft nur mit dem *Question paper* und übertragen Ihre Lösungen im Anschluss auf das *Answer sheet*. Die CD gibt Ihnen die genaue Zeit vor. Sie hören alle Teile zweimal, also keine Sorge, wenn Sie beim ersten Hören nicht alle Details verstanden haben. Einige Teile werden auch hier im *multiple choice*-Verfahren abgefragt, bei anderen müssen Sie selbst aus Gesprächen und Texten die richtigen Informationen heraushören und eintragen. Machen Sie sich unbedingt vorher mit den Aufgabenstellungen vertraut!

Der *Speaking*-Teil findet häufig für zwei Prüfungskandidaten gemeinsam statt und dauert etwa 8–10 Minuten. Er besteht aus zwei Teilen. Im ersten Teil werden Ihnen Fragen zu Ihrer Person gestellt (Freizeit, Hobbies, Schule/Beruf, Reisen, Familie, Haustiere, Freunde, Sport etc.). Im zweiten Teil bekommen Sie, je nach Anbieter, eine *prompt card* mit Informationen zu einem bestimmten Thema. Ihr Prüfungspartner stellt Ihnen dazu Fragen, die

Sie mit Hilfe der Informationen auf Ihrer Karte beantworten müssen. Im Anschluss daran tauschen Sie die Rollen und der andere Kandidat beantwortet Ihre Fragen. Sehen Sie sich hierzu die Anmerkungen zum *Speaking*-Test und den kompletten Testablauf in diesem Buch an.
Der Prüfungsinhalt besteht vorwiegend aus einfacheren Texten und alltäglichem Englisch. Üben Sie daher neben dem Unterricht mit Zeitungsausschnitten, Werbeanzeigen, Hinweistafeln, Gebrauchsanweisungen, Packungsbeilagen, Fahrplänen etc. Diese Materialien sind auch zur Vorbereitung auf die mündliche Prüfung ideal und Sie können gleichzeitig Ihren Wortschatz erweitern.

Wie kann man mit diesem Buch arbeiten?

In diesem Buch erhalten Sie einige allgemeine Hinweise und Tipps zur Bearbeitung Ihrer Sprachenzertifikats-Prüfung. Im Anschluss daran finden Sie fünf *Mock Exams*, mit denen Sie sich optimal auf die Aufgabenformen der Prüfung vorbereiten können. Bitte beachten Sie jedoch, dass die Prüfungen je nach Prüfungsanbieter etwas variieren können. Trotzdem ist es natürlich sinnvoll, sich im Voraus mit möglichen Aufgabenstellungen zu den verschiedenen Kompetenzbereichen vertraut zu machen. Dabei hilft Ihnen dieses Buch ganz besonders.
Sehen Sie sich zuerst die einzelnen Prüfungsteile an, damit Sie Routine in der Bearbeitung bekommen und wissen, worum es bei den jeweiligen Aufgaben geht und wie sie zu bearbeiten sind. Üben Sie mit den *Mock Exams* unter „realen Bedingungen", d. h. unter Einhaltung der entsprechenden Zeitvorgaben, damit Sie einschätzen können, wo Ihre Stärken und Schwächen liegen bzw. wie lange Sie für die einzelnen Aufgaben benötigen. Nutzen Sie die Vorlagen der *Answer sheets* und üben Sie auch das Übertragen, damit Sie in der Prüfung routiniert sind, nicht auf den Bögen herumsuchen müssen und wertvolle Zeit verlieren. Es zählen nur Ihre Antworten, die Sie auch tatsächlich auf dem Antwortbogen eingetragen haben. Selbstverständlich können Sie sich die Zeit selbst einteilen, d. h. Sie beginnen mit den Aufgaben, die Ihnen üblicherweise am besten gelingen oder die Sie am schnellsten bearbeiten können.

Weitere praktische Tipps

- Lassen Sie keinesfalls Aufgaben unbeantwortet, sondern verlassen Sie sich im Zweifelsfall auf Ihr „Bauchgefühl".
- Achten Sie beim Übertragen Ihrer Lösungen auf die Antwortbögen immer darauf, dass Ihre Antwort neben der richtigen Fragenummer steht.
- Üben Sie immer wieder das Buchstabieren von Namen und Begriffen; das kommt Ihnen sowohl im *Listening*- als auch im *Speaking*-Teil der Prüfung zu Gute.
- Halten Sie sich immer genau an die Aufgabenstellung (*write ONE word, write 25–35 words* etc.). Sollten Sie sich nicht mehr sicher sein, finden Sie die Arbeitsanweisung immer noch einmal am Anfang der Aufgabe.

- Schreiben Sie alles mit Bleistift. Sollten Sie etwas verbessern, radieren Sie es aus und stellen Sie sicher, dass Ihre Antworten auf dem Antwortbogen gut lesbar sind.
- Arbeiten Sie ruhig und konzentriert, ohne zu viele Pausen einzulegen. Vor der Abschlusskontrolle und der Übertragung der Lösungen auf den Antwortbogen sollten Sie sich aber noch einmal eine kurze Auszeit gönnen, um Ihren Kopf wieder frei zu bekommen und mögliche Fehler gezielt korrigieren zu können.

Und nun wünsche ich Ihnen viel Spaß beim Durcharbeiten der *Mock Exams* und vor allem viel Erfolg in Ihrer Prüfung!

Ihre

Michaela Kamm

Michaela Kamm

Tipps und Hinweise

Reading

multiple choice /multiple matching
Sehen Sie sich die Fragen genau an. Häufig kommen ähnliche Begriffe oder auch gleiche Wörter vor. Prüfen Sie immer den Inhalt der Aussage. Sobald Sie meinen die richtige Antwort gefunden zu haben, wägen Sie noch einmal ab, ob es eine noch genauer zutreffende Lösung gibt.

Lückentext
Versuchen Sie der Reihe nach die Lücken mit den besten Lösungen zu füllen. Oft erscheinen zwei Antworten möglich. Notieren Sie erst einmal beide, meist passt eine davon noch besser in eine Lücke weiter unten. Prüfen Sie immer den vorhergehenden und den folgenden Satz. Die Lösung muss sich sowohl grammatikalisch als auch inhaltlich gut einfügen.

right / wrong / dosn't say
Hier gibt es zwei mögliche Formate.
Sollen Sie sich zwischen „right", „wrong" oder „doesn't say" entscheiden, gehen Sie nach folgendem Prinzip vor: „Right" – steht so im Text. „Wrong" – wird im Text erwähnt, aber Aussage ist falsch. „Doesn't say" – die Aussage wird im Text nicht erwähnt oder reicht nicht aus, um sich für „right" oder „wrong" zu entscheiden. Lesen Sie immer die Frage genau, es kann sein dass eine Aussage vielleicht allgemein richtig ist, sich aber im Textzusammenhang als falsch herausstellt.
Beim zweiten Format sollen Sie sich für eine von drei Aussagen entscheiden. Dabei ist es ebenfalls wichtig, die Frage ganz genau zu lesen, da die drei vorgegebenen Aussagen sich oft nur geringfügig voneinander unterscheiden!

Fill in ...
Achten Sie genau auf die Fragestellung und die verfügbaren Informationen. Häufig kommen mehrere Daten, Zeitangaben, Preise oder Telefonnummern vor. Prüfen Sie exakt, wonach gefragt wird.

Writing

Schreiben Sie kurze, übersichtliche Sätze und schließen Sie unbedingt alle drei Punkte ein. Bei dieser Aufgabe können Sie eine „Note" zwischen 0 (absolut unverständlich) und maximal 5 (alle drei Punkte klar verständlich, nur minimale Grammatik- und Rechtschreibfehler) erzielen. Ihr Schreiben muss nicht perfekt sein, aber den allgemeinen Regeln (z. B. Anrede und Ihre Unterschrift am Ende eines E-mails/einer Mitteilung) entsprechen. Benutzen Sie nur Wörter und Wendungen, die Sie sicher beherrschen und machen Sie in der Prüfung keine Experimente mit schwierigen Begriffen. Halten Sie sich unbedingt an die vorgegebene Länge, d. h. schreiben Sie mindestens 25 (bei weniger gibt es Punktabzug) und höchstens ca. 35 Wörter. Schreiben Sie deutlich in Ihrer Handschrift, nur was gelesen werden kann, kann auch korrigiert werden!

Listening

Kreuzen Sie beim ersten Zuhören die Antwort an, die Sie für richtig halten und versuchen Sie beim zweiten Durchgang auf alle Einzelheiten zu achten. Häufig werden mehrere in den Lösungen vorkommende Wörter erwähnt. Lesen Sie die Frage nochmals genau durch und versuchen Sie beim zweiten Mal die beste Lösung zu finden. Sollten Sie etwas auch beim zweiten Hören nicht verstanden haben, versuchen Sie die Lösung aus dem zuvor und danach Gesagten zu erschließen. Oft hilft Ihnen logisches Kombinieren auch weiter. Arbeiten Sie nur mit dem *Question paper* und übertragen Sie Ihre Antworten danach auf das *Answer sheet.*

Speaking

Der *Speaking*-Teil dauert etwa 8–10 Minuten und besteht aus zwei Teilen. Im ersten Teil, einem kurzen Interview, stellt der Prüfer einige persönliche Fragen. Sie sollten Auskunft geben können über alltägliche Dinge wie z. B.

- Schule/Arbeit
- Ihren Namen (den Sie meist auch buchstabieren müssen)
- Hobbies/Interessen
- Sport
- Freunde
- Wohnort
- Familie
- Freizeit/Urlaub

Denken Sie daran, dass Ihre Antworten nicht unbedingt der Wahrheit entsprechen müssen. Wenn Ihnen gerade das Wort für Ihren Lieblingssport oder ein Leibgericht nicht einfällt, dann nehmen Sie einfach etwas anderes. Es kommt in erster Linie darauf an, das Gespräch authentisch fortzuführen. Geben Sie so viele Informationen wie möglich, auch wenn Sie sonst vielleicht eher schüchtern sind …

Im zweiten Teil erhalten Sie *prompt cards* zu einem bestimmten Thema. Sie stellen Fragen dazu und Ihr Prüfungspartner antwortet Ihnen. Danach werden die Rollen getauscht und Sie beantworten die Fragen Ihres Partners zu einem anderen Thema. Dieser Prüfungsteil lässt sich sehr gut vorbereiten. Üben Sie bestimmte Redewendungen um Details zu erfragen, z. B.

- *When does it start?*
- *How much is it?*
- *What does it cost?*

- *Is there a special price for (children/students)?*
- *Can you tell me more about ...?*
- *How far is it to ...?*
- *Where is ... located?*
- *Are there (any) ...?*

Ob Ihnen für den *Speaking*-Teil eine Vorbereitungszeit gewährt wird, hängt vom Anbieter der Prüfung ab. Es werden meist zwei Kandidaten zusammen geprüft. Einer der Prüfer unterhält sich mit Ihnen, der zweite hört zu. Sie bekommen vor der mündlichen Prüfung *Mark sheets*, zur Weitergaben an die Prüfer. Sie brauchen auf den *Mark sheets* nichts einzutragen; geben Sie sie einfach auf Verlangen an den Prüfer. Versuchen Sie die Fragen so genau wie möglich zu beantworten und immer zu begründen. Wenn Ihnen ein Wort fehlt, ersetzen Sie es durch einen ähnlichen Begriff oder umschreiben Sie es und sprechen einfach weiter. Neben Vokabelkenntnissen und Grammatik wird auch bewertet, wie gut Sie mit Ihrem Partner bzw. dem Prüfer zusammenarbeiten bzw. ob Sie versuchen die Fragen zu beantworten, um zu einem Ergebnis zu kommen.
Beide Kandidaten werden getrennt voneinander von beiden Prüfern anhand der Vorgaben für das Prüfungsniveau A 2 bewertet. Der Prüfer mit dem Sie sprechen, gibt Ihnen eine Gesamtnote, während der beisitzende Prüfer Grammatik, Vokabelkenntnisse, Aussprache und interaktive Kommunikation bewertet.
Üben Sie unbedingt vorher, wenn möglich mit einem Partner, das nimmt Ihnen die Nervosität und bereitet Sie optimal auf den *Speaking*-Test vor. Arbeiten Sie immer wieder mit den *prompt cards* aus diesem Buch und prägen Sie sich die Redewendungen, die Sie brauchen, um die Fragen zu stellen bzw. zu beantworten, gut ein. Spielen Sie die Situation immer wieder durch, im Idealfall mit weiteren Prüfungsteilnehmern. Es lohnt sich auf jeden Fall im Vorfeld etwas zu üben!

▶ Übungsaufgaben zum Sprachenzertifikat

Sprachenzertifikat Englisch A2
Mock Exam 1

Paper 1: Reading and Writing

Part 1

Questions 1–5
*Which notice (**A–H**) says this (**1–5**)?*
*For questions 1–5, mark the correct letters **A–H** on your answer sheet.*

Example:

0. You can use only this service only at weekends. [D]

1. Contact this person if you want a weekend job. [ ]
2. This door is only for people who work here. [ ]
3. There is a special price for children. [ ]
4. This service will be more expensive next week. [ ]
5. Call this number if you need information about the weather. [ ]

A campsite gates closed from 11.00 p.m.

B Telephone:
52949 for weather forecast
89270 for transportation service

C Please return library books by Thursday
The office is closed this Friday

D **Hotel Shuttle Bus**
Friday, Saturday, Sunday

E newspaper advertisements
15 % special discount
this week only

F **Entrance for hotel staff only!**

G Outdoor Funpark
Open every afternoon
Adults £ 3.00
Children: £ 1.00

H Waiter needed for Fri./Sat.
Email: Susi.Wong@xyz.com

Part 2

Questions 6–10
Read the sentences about making a birthday cake.
*Choose the best word (**A, B** or **C**) for each space.*
*For questions 6–10, mark **A**, **B** or **C** on your answer sheet.*

Example:

0. Sarah was … for a present for her mother.

   A ☐ trying **B** ☑ looking **C** ☐ finding

6. Sarah … to make a cake for her mother's birthday.

   A ☐ wanted **B** ☐ thought **C** ☐ liked

7. First she … everything she needed.

   A ☐ sold **B** ☐ returned **C** ☐ bought

8. At home, her little sister … to help her.

   A ☐ invited **B** ☐ decided **C** ☐ pleased

9. When the cake was nearly …, the girls saw the sugar still standing on the kitchen table.

   A ☐ ended **B** ☐ finish **C** ☐ ready

10. In the end, Sarah went to the shop round the … and bought a lovely cake for her mother.

    A ☐ corner **B** ☐ town **C** ☐ square

Part 3

Questions 11–15
Complete the five conversations.
*For questions 11–15, mark **A**, **B** or **C** on your answer sheet.*

Example:

0. Did you understand what the teacher said?

   A ☐ Nothing special.
   B ☑ Not really.
   C ☐ It's not enough.

11. Thank you for the information.

    A ☐ Please.
    B ☐ Don't worry.
    C ☐ You're welcome.

12. Would you like another drink?
- **A** ☐ Yes, once more.
- **B** ☐ I'll have it.
- **C** ☐ A cup of coffee would be nice.

13. Peter is going to stay with us in the summer.
- **A** ☐ How long for?
- **B** ☐ How many?
- **C** ☐ How is he?

14. Can you take a photo of us?
- **A** ☐ Yes, please.
- **B** ☐ Yes, no problem.
- **C** ☐ Not at all.

15. Nice to see you again.
- **A** ☐ Pleased to meet you, too.
- **B** ☐ Nice to see you, too.
- **C** ☐ How do you do?

Questions 16–20
Complete the conversation about shopping.
What does Ken say to Oliver?
*For questions 16–20, mark the correct letter **A–H** on your answer sheet.*

Example:

Ken: Hello Oliver. What are you doing this afternoon?

Oliver: **0.** F

Ken: Can you go shopping with me?

Oliver: **16.** _______

Ken: Well, I need a birthday present for my sister and I don't know what to get her.

Oliver: **17.** _______

Ken: I think the new department store in Fletcher Street might be a good idea.

Oliver: **18.** _______

Ken: Okay, but I think it's a bit far to walk. Shall we take the bus?

Oliver: **19.** _______

A Yes, let's meet at the bus station at twenty to three.

B Yes, why not. What do you want to buy?

C It's not that easy, you know.

D Finding presents for little girls isn't easy at all! Where do you want to go?

E Not yet. I still have maths to do and I think it's really difficult!

F Nothing special, why are you asking?

G I don't think so. It's too far to walk.

Ken:	Alright. Have you finished all your homework for tomorrow?	**H**	Yes, that sounds good. They have a large toy department, too.
Oliver:	**20.** _______		
Ken:	We can do it together if you like. It's quite easy, I'll help you.		

Part 4

Questions 21–27
Read the text about a film that was shown on TV.
*Are the sentences 21–27 'Right' (**A**) or 'Wrong' (**B**)?*
*If there is not enough information to answer 'Right' (**A**) or 'Wrong' (**B**), choose 'Doesn't say' (**C**).*
*For questions 21–27, mark **A**, **B** or **C** on your answer sheet.*

When I was a child of about 11 years I watched a serial on TV which I found very exciting. It was a detective story set in a small Norwegian village in winter. Three children were watching a young man and his girlfriend who had moved to the village not long ago. Nobody knew why the strangers had come to the village or what they were doing during the day.

When it got dark they walked around and often went to the ruins of an old factory a few miles outside the village. The children had sometimes seen them there and wanted to find out what the young man and woman were looking for.

I can still remember some of the most exciting black and white scenes of the two or three parts I watched. However, I missed the last two parts of the film and never found out how it ended. I looked in all the TV magazines and hoped to find the serial. After some time I gave up and never heard anything about it for the next 30 years.

But, what a surprise when I started my computer last week! There was an advertisement for the film, which is now available on DVD! I immediately ordered it online and now I can't wait to find out how the story ends!

Example:

0. The writer watched some parts of the serial when she was about 11 years old.

A ☑ Right **B** ☐ Wrong **C** ☐ Doesn't say

21. The writer saw the film at the cinema.

A ☐ Right **B** ☐ Wrong **C** ☐ Doesn't say

22. The people in the village did not know where the young man and woman worked.
    A ☐ Right **B** ☐ Wrong **C** ☐ Doesn't say

23. Many people watched the film in Norway.
    A ☐ Right **B** ☐ Wrong **C** ☐ Doesn't say

24. The young man and his girlfriend often went to the ruins of an old castle at night.
    A ☐ Right **B** ☐ Wrong **C** ☐ Doesn't say

25. The writer watched five parts of the film.
    A ☐ Right **B** ☐ Wrong **C** ☐ Doesn't say

26. The writer ordered a DVD when she saw an advertisement for the film.
    A ☐ Right **B** ☐ Wrong **C** ☐ Doesn't say

27. The DVD will be sent by post.
    A ☐ Right **B** ☐ Wrong **C** ☐ Doesn't say

Part 5

Questions 28–35
*Read the article about the castles. Choose the best answer (**A**, **B** or **C**) for each space.*
*For answers 28–35, mark **A**, **B** or **C** on your answer sheet.*

Castles

Apart from churches, castles (0) ________ the oldest buildings we can still see today. Some are more (28) ________ 1, 000 years old and were built during the Middle Ages. The castles protected the people (29) ________ lived there or were the normal homes of the knights and (30) ______ families. The farmers and people who (31) _______ around the castle belonged to the owner of the castle just like the animals, the forest and the land. Inside the thick walls (32) ______ the castle you could find everything the knight and his family (33) _____ to survive for some time when they were under attack. When we see (34) ______ ruins today, we think of fights, dragons and cold winters. However, it is not easy to imagine the normal life of the people who lived (35) ______ long ago!

Example:

0.	**A** ☐ is	**B** ☑ are	**C** ☐ were
28.	**A** ☐ their	**B** ☐ over	**C** ☐ than
29.	**A** ☐ who	**B** ☐ which	**C** ☐ they
30.	**A** ☐ them	**B** ☐ their	**C** ☐ his
31.	**A** ☐ living	**B** ☐ lives	**C** ☐ lived
32.	**A** ☐ of	**B** ☐ from	**C** ☐ about
33.	**A** ☐ need	**B** ☐ needed	**C** ☐ needs
34.	**A** ☐ them	**B** ☐ the	**C** ☐ any
35.	**A** ☐ such	**B** ☐ some	**C** ☐ so

Part 6

Questions 36–40
Read the descriptions of some things you can see in an office.
What is the word for each one?
The first letter is already there. There is one space for each other letter in the word.
For questions 36 – 40, write the words on your answer sheet.

Example:

0. The table where you work — d e s k.

36. You need these to cut something up, for example paper. — s _ _ _ _ _ _ _ _

37. On your computer, you type emails and letters on the — k _ _ _ _ _ _ _ _.

38. If you want to look up an English word you can use a — d _ _ _ _ _ _ _ _ _ _ _.

39. To find out today's date, you look on the — c _ _ _ _ _ _ _ _.

40. Before you post a letter, you put it in an — e _ _ _ _ _ _ _ _.

Part 7

Questions 41–50
Complete the information Bob wrote for the school exchange programme.
*Write **one** word for each space.*
For questions 41–50, write the words on your answer sheet.

Example: (**0**) *name*

Hello,

My (**0**) *name* is Bob Hunter and I (**41**) ______________ fifteen years old. I come (**42**) ______________ Munich in Germany. I live in a nice flat (**43**) ______________ my parents and my little sister, Petra. My favourite subject (**44**) ______________ school is maths. When I grow up, I want to (**45**) ______________ a pilot. I (**46**) ______________ like to see many different countries and cities. My parents like gardening and usually (**47**) ______________ at home in the summer. Therefore, I (**48**) ______________ only been on holiday in winter so far. This year, however, I am going (**49**) ______________ fly to Spain with my grandparents. I'm really looking (**50**) ______________ to it.

Part 8

Questions 51–55
Read the note and the letter about music lessons at school.
Fill in the information on the booking form.
For questions 51–55, write the information on your answer sheet.

12th August

Dear students,

Music lessons at our school will start again in September. The cost this year is £ **25** per course. Last year it was £ 20.

Piano lessons are on **Monday** from 4 to 5.30 pm and **guitar lessons** on **Tuesday** at the same time.

There is another piano course on Thursday at 3 o'clock this year (many of you have French lessons on Monday afternoon).

Please return form by Friday!

Peter Dawson

Dear Susan,

Can you please fill in my form?
I am not at school today because I'm visiting a factory with my new class, 4c.
I want to take piano lessons but we have French classes on Monday afternoon!
It's a pity, I'm no longer in your class!

See you on Monday,

Hannah Miller

MUSIC LESSONS BOOKING FORM

Name:	51	
Class:	52	
Instrument:	53	
Day and Time of Lesson:	54	______________ 3 pm
Cost:	55	£ ______________

Part 9

Question 56
You are going to help on a farm this afternoon. Your friend Tom wants to come, too.
Write an email to Tom.

Say:
- what clothes to wear
- what work you can do
- what time you want to go

Write 25–35 words.
Write the e- mail on your answer sheet.

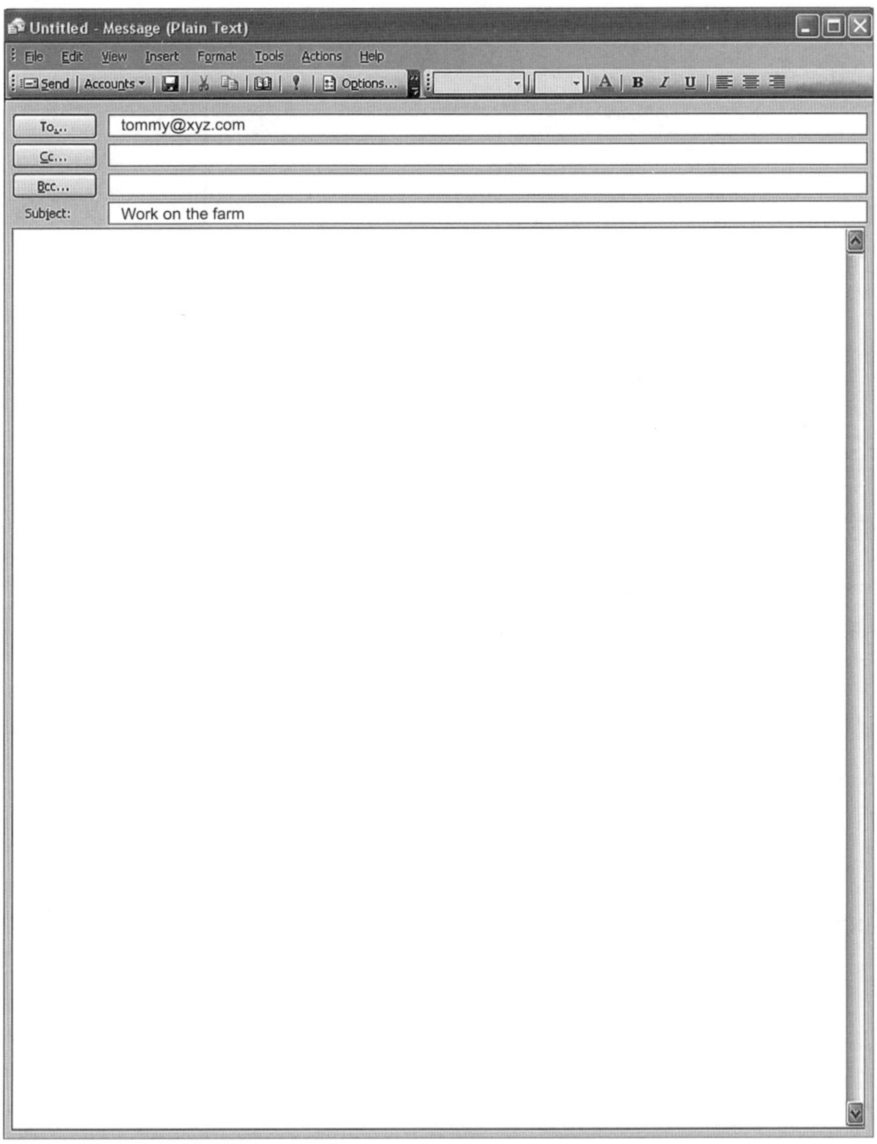

Paper 2: Listening

Part 1

Tracks
1–5

You will hear five short conversations.
You will hear each conversation twice.
There is one question for each conversation.
For questions 1–5, put a tick (✓) under the right answer.

Example:

0. When did the concert start?

WOMAN: Did the concert start at three o'clock yesterday?

MAN: No, they had planned to start at three thirty but the bus was late so they started at four.

A ☐

B ☐

C ☑

1. What is Rita going to do in the afternoon?

A ☐

B ☐

C ☐

2. Which lamp does Helen choose?

A ☐

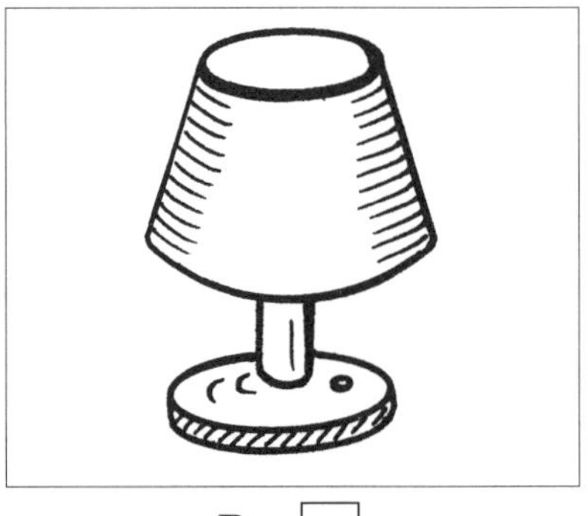

B ☐

C ☐

3. Which boy is Paul's brother?

A ☐

B ☐

C ☐

4. What time do they leave?

A ☐

B ☐

C ☐

5. What did the friends do last Saturday?

A ☐

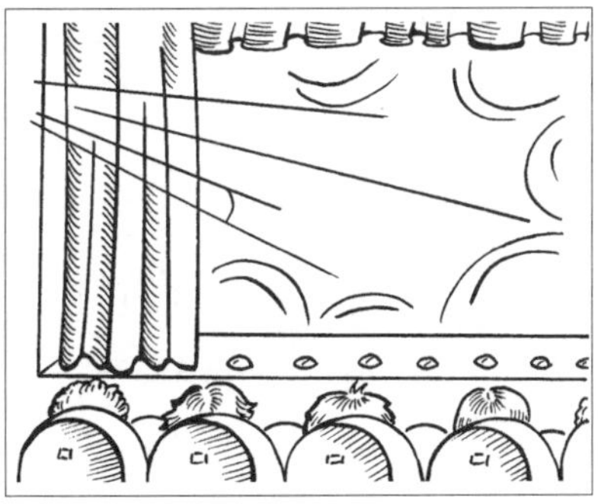

B ☐

C ☐

Part 2

Track 6

Questions 6–10
Listen to Rachel telling her grandfather about special projects at school each month.
Which projects have they done this year?
*For questions 6–10, write a letter (**A–H**) next to each month.*
You will hear the conversation twice.

Example:

0.	Januar	F	**A**	Concert
6.	February	☐	**B**	Dinner
7.	March	☐	**C**	Art exhibition
8.	April	☐	**D**	Camping
9.	May	☐	**E**	Website
10.	June	☐	**F**	Animals
			G	Factory
			H	Outdoor museum

Part 3

Track 7

Questions 11–15
Listen to Frances and Sam talking about a new leisure centre.
*For questions 11–15, tick (✓) **A**, **B** or **C**.*
You will hear the conversation twice.

Example:

0. The name of the centre is
   A ☐ Sports and Leisure.
   B ☐ Leisure and Fun.
   C ✓ Fun and Sports.

11. The centre is in
    A ☐ a park.
    B ☐ the city centre.
    C ☐ Greenfield Estate.

12. What is **not** possible at the centre?
    A ☐ Making music
    B ☐ Table tennis
    C ☐ Ice-skating

13. The card for teenagers costs
- **A** ☐ £20
- **B** ☐ £15
- **C** ☐ £25

14. The kids' club is only for children under
- **A** ☐ nine.
- **B** ☐ eleven.
- **C** ☐ eighteen.

15. Sam's favourite sport is
- **A** ☐ ice-skating.
- **B** ☐ swimming.
- **C** ☐ mountain-biking.

Track 8

Part 4

Questions 16–20
You will hear a conversation at a ticket agency.
Listen and complete questions 16–20.
You will hear the conversation twice.

WILD ONES TICKETS		
Day:	**16**	______________
Price:	**17**	£ ______________
Number of tickets:	**18**	______________
Name:	**19**	Henry ______________
Will collect tickets on:	**20**	______________

Part 5

Track 9

Questions 21–25
You will hear a man leaving a message about a camping site.
Listen and complete questions 21–25.
You will hear the information twice.

Camping Site		
This year open from (month)	**21**	______________
Minimum stay on weekends:	**22**	______________
Camping site has	**23**	______________ RENTAL
Office hours:	**24**	2 PM – ______________ PM
Booking Hotline:	**25**	______________

You now have 8 minutes to write your answers on the answer sheet.

Paper 3: Speaking

Part 1

Part 1 consists of a short conversation with the examiner. You should be familiar with the language associated with meeting people for the first time and you should be able to give information of a personal kind, e. g name, place of origin, occupation, family etc. You are also expected to talk about your daily life, your hobbies etc.

Part 2

Prompt cards are used to stimulate questions and answers. The examiner gives instructions and hands out a questions card to one candidate and an answer card to the other. After the candidates have asked and answered their questions, they change roles.

Example

The examiner gives a question card to Candidate B and an answer card to Candidate A.

Candidate A, here is some information about origami lessons.

Candidate B, you don't know anything about these lessons, so ask A some questions about it. Now B, ask A your questions about the origami lessons and A, you answer them.

Candidate A – your information.

Origami Lessons

Mondays 2 pm
Lessons free · £5 for material
Classroom 251 (second floor)
Teacher: Ms Fletcher
Bring: scissors and pencil

Candidate B – your questions.

Origami Lessons

- When?
- Teacher?
- Cost?
- Bring anything?
- Where?

Candidate B, here is some information about jobs for students.

Candidate A, you don't know anything about these jobs, so ask B some questions about them. Now A, ask B your questions about the jobs and B, you answer them.

Candidate B – your information.

Jobs for students

HOTEL BREEZY LAKE

We need help in the kitchen

Friday - Sunday 5 - 9 pm · £7 per hour

Contact Helen:
Helbreezy@wex.uk or call 271 473

Candidate A – your questions.

Jobs for students

- Where/job?
- What/job?
- How much?
- When/work?
- Telephone?

Lösungsvorschläge

Reading and Writing

Part 1

1. Contact this person if you want a weekend job. **H**
2. This door is only for people who work here. **F**
3. There is a special price for children. **G**
4. This service will be more expensive next week. **E**
5. Call this number if you need information about the weather. **B**

Part 2

6. Sarah … to make a cake for her mother's birthday.
   A ☑ wanted **B** ☐ thought **C** ☐ liked

7. First she … everything she needed.
   A ☐ sold **B** ☐ returned **C** ☑ bought

8. At home, her little sister … to help her.
   A ☐ invited **B** ☑ decided **C** ☐ pleased

9. When the cake was nearly …, the girls saw the sugar still standing on the kitchen table.
   A ☐ ended **B** ☐ finish **C** ☑ ready

10. In the end, Sarah went to the shop round the … and bought a lovely cake for her mother.
    A ☑ corner **B** ☐ town **C** ☐ square

Part 3

11. Thank you for the information.
    A ☐ Please.
    B ☐ Don't worry.
    C ☑ You're welcome.

12. Would you like another drink?
    A ☐ Yes, once more.
    B ☐ I'll have it.
    C ☑ A cup of coffee would be nice.

13. Peter is going to stay with us in the summer.
- A ☑ How long for?
- B ☐ How many?
- C ☐ How is he?

14. Can you take a photo of us?
- A ☐ Yes, please.
- B ☑ Yes, no problem.
- C ☐ Not at all.

15. Nice to see you again.
- A ☐ Pleased to meet you, too.
- B ☑ Nice to see you, too.
- C ☐ How do you do?

Ken: Can you go shopping with me?
Oliver: **16.** B

Ken: Well, I need a birthday present for my sister and I don't know what to get her.
Oliver: **17.** D

Ken: I think the new department store in Fletcher Street might be a good idea.
Oliver: **18.** H

Ken: Okay, but I think it's a bit far to walk. Shall we take the bus?
Oliver: **19.** A

Ken: Alright. Have you finished all your homework for tomorrow?
Oliver: **20.** E
Ken: We can do it together if you like. It's quite easy, I'll help you.

Part 4

21. The writer saw the film at the cinema.
A ☐ Right **B** ☑ Wrong **C** ☐ Doesn't say

22. The people in the village did not know where the young man and woman worked.
A ☑ Right **B** ☐ Wrong **C** ☐ Doesn't say

23. Many people watched the film in Norway.
A ☐ Right **B** ☐ Wrong **C** ☑ Doesn't say

24. The young man and his girlfriend often went to the ruins of an old castle at night.
A ☐ Right **B** ☑ Wrong **C** ☐ Doesn't say

25. The writer watched five parts of the film.
    A ☐ Right **B** ☑ Wrong **C** ☐ Doesn't say

26. The writer ordered a DVD when she saw an advertisement for the film.
    A ☑ Right **B** ☐ Wrong **C** ☐ Doesn't say

27. The DVD will be sent by post.
    A ☐ Right **B** ☐ Wrong **C** ☑ Doesn't say

Part 5

28. **A** ☐ their **B** ☐ over **C** ☑ than

29. **A** ☑ who **B** ☐ which **C** ☐ they

30. **A** ☐ them **B** ☑ their **C** ☐ his

31. **A** ☐ living **B** ☐ lives **C** ☑ lived

32. **A** ☑ of **B** ☐ from **C** ☐ about

33. **A** ☐ need **B** ☑ needed **C** ☐ needs

34. **A** ☐ them **B** ☑ the **C** ☐ any

35. **A** ☐ such **B** ☐ some **C** ☑ so

Part 6

36. You need these to cut something up, for example paper. **scissors**

37. On your computer, you type emails and letters on the **keyboard**.

38. If you want to look up an English word you can use a **dictionary**.

39. To find out today's date, you look on the **calendar**.

40. Before you post a letter, you put it in an **envelope**.

Part 7

Hello,
My (**0**) name is Bob Hunter and I (**41**) **am/'m** fifteen years old. I come (**42**) **from** Munich in Germany. I live in a nice flat (**43**) **with** my parents and my little sister, Petra. My favourite subject (**44**) **at** school is maths. When I grow up, I want to (**45**) **be/become** a pilot.
I (**46**) **would/'d** like to see many different countries and cities. My parents like gardening and usually (**47**) **stay/are** at home in the summer. Therefore, I (**48**) **have** only been on holiday in winter so far. This year, however, I am going (**49**) **to** fly to Spain with my grandparents. I'm really looking (**50**) **forward** to it.

Part 8

Name:	51	Hannah Miller
Class:	52	4 c
Instrument:	53	piano
Day and Time of Lesson:	54	Thursday 3 pm
Cost:	55	£25

Part 9

Hinweis: *Es müssen alle* ***drei Punkte*** *behandelt werden. Das Schreiben* ***muss mindestens 25 Wörter*** *lang sein.*

Hello Tom,
It's great that you are coming to the farm with me. You should wear old clothes. I think we can help the farmer with the animals or in his vegetable garden. Let's meet at my house at 3 o'clock. I'm looking forward to seeing you.
Peter

Listening

Part 1

Tracks 1–5

1. **What is Rita going to do in the afternoon?**
   MAN: Hi Rita, we're going ice-skating in the afternoon. Are you coming, too?
   WOMAN: I'd love to but I've got a cold.
   MAN: You could come later and have coffee with us.
   WOMAN: No, sorry. I have to take some books back to the library.

2. **Which lamp does Helen choose?**
   WOMAN: I want to buy a new lamp for my bedroom. I think the small one is very nice.
   MAN: Yes, it is but I don't like the stars. I think they are a bit childish.
   WOMAN: Hm, you're right. I'll take the other one then.

3. **Which boy is Paul's brother?**
   WOMAN: Is that your brother over there?
   MAN: Oh yes, I didn't even know he was here.
   WOMAN: What a nice suit he's wearing! And he's wearing a really nice tie today, too.
   MAN: Yes, I'm glad he's not wearing the one with the elephants on it!

4. **What time do they leave?**
   MAN: Have you got everything for the party?
   WOMAN: I think so. Are we taking the train at 4.30?
   MAN: No, we can catch the five o'clock bus.
   WOMAN: I don't like that bus, it's always so full. Let's go by car.
   MAN: Alright. If we take the car we can leave at 5.30.
   WOMAN: That's good because I need to get a present.

5. **What did the friends do last Saturday?**
   BOY: Did you go swimming with Tim and Polly on Saturday?
   GIRL: We wanted to but the pool was closed for repairs.
   BOY: Oh, dear! So what did you do then?
   GIRL: Well, first Tim suggested playing table tennis but in the end we went to see the new James Bond film.

1. What is Rita going to do in the afternoon?

A ☐

B ☐

C ☑

2. Which lamp does Helen choose?

A ☐

B ☑

C ☐

3. Which boy is Paul's brother?

A ☐

B ☐

C ☑

4. What time do they leave?

A ☑

B ☐

C ☐

5. What did the friends do last Saturday?

A ☐

B ☑

C ☐

Track 6

Part 2

GRANDPA: Tell me about the special projects you're doing at school, Rachel.

RACHEL: Well, this year it's really interesting. In January we brought all our pets to school in the Biology lesson. It was great fun!

GRANDPA: I can imagine! What was next?

RACHEL: In February we wanted to go to the outdoor museum to look at old buildings but it was snowing a lot so we couldn't go. Mr Henderson decided to update the school website with us.

GRANDPA: Oh, that sounds good. You can help me with the family website I'm planning.

RACHEL: Yes, I'd love to. Anyway, in March we had to choose between a concert and an art exhibition in the town hall. I decided to paint a nice picture because I don't play an instrument.

GRANDPA: Hm, I prefer painting to making music, too. What did you do in April?

RACHEL: That was a really exciting project! We prepared a dinner in the school kitchen and invited our parents.

GRANDPA: You should have invited your grandparents as well!

RACHEL: Well, maybe next time. So, let me think, in May we visited a local factory. That was really interesting: we had a look at the production first and later there was ice-cream for everyone in the canteen!

GRANDPA: What a pity we didn't do things like that when I went to school!

RACHEL: Yes, must have been pretty boring then. Oh, and in June the weather was really good so we finally visited the outdoor museum. I enjoyed it a lot because we were allowed to try all the old things!

GRANDPA: School really seems to be fun nowadays.

RACHEL: Well, not all the time!

6. February **E**
7. March **C**
8. April **B**
9. May **G**
10. June **H**

Part 3

Track 7

FRANCES: Hi Sam. What are you doing?

SAM: Hello Frances. I'm on my way to the new leisure centre.

FRANCES: Which one? I haven't heard about it.

SAM: Oh, really? It's called Fun and Sports and it's absolutely fantastic.

FRANCES: Is it the one in Greenfield Estate? I read about it in the newspaper.

SAM: No, it's right in the city centre, so it's quite easy to get to. You just have to cycle or walk through the park.

FRANCES: What can you do there?

SAM: Well, lots of things really. Swimming, bowling, ice-skating and so on. They even have a room there where you can make music with your friends. And there are nice cafés and a small Italian restaurant.

FRANCES: Wow, sounds great. Is it expensive?

SAM: It's not exactly cheap but you can get a card for £25, I think, and go there as often as you want. For teenagers up to eighteen the card is even cheaper, only £20 for one month. You can use nearly everything and you can bring one child under eleven years to the kids' club for free.

FRANCES: Great. That means I could go ice-skating instead of looking after my little brother. Ice-skating's my favourite sport, you know. What's yours?

SAM: Well, it's one of the few things you can't do at the new centre – mountain-biking.

11. The centre is in
A ☐ a park.
B ☑ the city centre.
C ☐ Greenfield Estate.

12. What is **not** possible at the centre?
A ☐ Making music
B ☑ Table tennis
C ☐ Ice-skating

13. The card for teenagers costs
A ☑ £20.
B ☐ £15.
C ☐ £25.

14. The kids' club is only for children under
A ☐ nine.
B ☑ eleven.
C ☐ eighteen.

15. Sam's favourite sport is
A ☐ ice-skating.
B ☐ swimming.
C ☑ mountain-biking.

Part 4

Track 8

BOY: Hello. I'd like to buy tickets for the Wild Ones concert next Saturday.

WOMAN: I'm sorry, but there are no tickets left for Saturday. I have some tickets for Sunday if that's OK for you.

BOY: OK, I'll take them. How much are they?

WOMAN: They're only £27 instead of £30 for the Saturday tickets.

BOY: Oh, that's good news.

WOMAN: How many would you like?

BOY: I need three, please. Oh, Peter's coming now as well, so it'll be four altogether.

WOMAN: OK, four then. Can I take your name and telephone number, please?

BOY: It's Henry Laughton, and the phone number is 8975421.

WOMAN: Could you spell your name for me, please?

BOY: Of course. It's L-A-U-G-H-T-O-N.

WOMAN: Can you pick up the tickets some time next week or should I send them?

BOY: No, you don't need to send them. I'll collect them next Tuesday. Thank you.

WOMAN: Thank you. Bye.

BOY: Goodbye.

Day:	16	Sunday
Price:	17	£27
Number of tickets:	18	4
Name:	19	Henry Laughton
Will collect tickets on:	20	Tuesday

Part 5

Track 9

Good afternoon, this is the Best Holiday Camping Site. You have asked us to give you some information. Well, we open in May this year, not in April as it says in last year's brochure. You can book per night or per week. On weekends we only take bookings for a minimum of two nights, though. Of course there is a price reduction if you stay for a week or more.

There are some shops here; we even have a small supermarket and you can rent bicycles. You cannot rent caravans or boats, however.

If you need further information you can call us on 1232-347574. Our office hours are from 2 pm – 5.30 pm. If you want to make a reservation, please call our booking hotline on 887592 at any time during the day.

This year open from (month)	21	May
Minimum stay on weekends:	22	2 nights
Camping site has	23	bicycle RENTAL
Office hours:	24	2 PM – 5.30 PM
Booking Hotline:	25	887592

Speaking

Part 1

PRÜFER: Good afternoon. Can I have your mark sheets? I am XY and this is my colleague XYZ.
zu Kandidat 1: What's your name?
Kandidat 1: My name is Ella.
zu Kandidat 2: And what is your name?
KANDIAT 2: My name is Sergej Kranz.
zu Kandidat 1: And what's your surname?
KANDIDAT 1: My family name is Hauser.
PRÜFER: And how do you spell that?
ELLA: H – A – U – S – E – R.
PRÜFER: Sergej, can you spell your last name?
SERGEJ: Yes, it's K – R – A – N – Z.

***Hinweis:** Der Prüfer stellt den Kandidaten nun abwechselnd persönliche Fragen. Dieser Teil der Prüfung dauert insgesamt 5–6 Minuten. Hier sind einige Beispiele mit möglichen Antworten.*

Do you work or are you a student?
(I'm a student. I attend XY school here in Munich.)

Where do you live?
(I live in Starnberg near Munich.)

What is your favourite food?
(I love Italian food, especially spaghetti.)

Do you like watching TV?
(Not very much, I prefer reading.)

What did you do last weekend?
(I went to a concert in Frankfurt.)

Where do you usually go on holiday?
(We sometimes travel to Spain. My aunt lives there.)

What do you think of (your town)?
(I really like living here. It's a nice place.)

Do you study English at school?
(Yes, we have 4 English lessons a week.)

Which is your favourite animal?
(I like cats best.)

Und dann einige Fragen, bei denen Sie etwas längere Antworten geben können:

Tell me something about ....
... your hobbies.
(In my free time I play Basketball in a team. I like it a lot because most of my friends play in this team, too.)
(I like painting. We have art lessons every Tuesday at school. It's my favourite day of the week.
... the clothes you like.
(I like sports clothes and jeans because they're very comfortable. They look good, too.)

Part 2

Hinweis: *Die Informationen in Klammern sind nicht unbedingt nötig. Sie können aber jederzeit Zusatzinformationen einbauen, falls Ihnen gerade etwas Passendes einfällt. Selbstverständlich gibt es hier viele Möglichkeiten, die Fragen zu stellen und zu beantworten. Es ist möglich, dass der Prüfer Sie unterbricht, obwohl Sie noch nicht alle Fragen gestellt/beantwortet haben. Dieser Prüfungsteil dauert insgesamt nur 3–4 Minuten, die häufig recht schnell vergehen.*

PRÜFER: Ella, here is some information about **Origami lessons**. Sergej, you don't know anything about Origami lessons, so ask Ella some questions about them. Now Sergej, ask your questions and Ella you answer them.
SERGEJ (CANDIDATE B): Ella, can you tell me when the Origami lessons start?
ELLA (CANDIDATE A): They start on Monday at 2 pm.
SERGEJ (CANDIDATE B): And who is the teacher?
ELLA (CANDIDATE A): The teacher is Ms Fletcher, our English teacher.
SERGEJ (CANDIDATE B): And how much are the lessons?
ELLA (CANDIDATE A): Well the lessons are free but you must pay 5 pounds for the material.
SERGEJ (CANDIDATE B): Do I need to bring anything?
ELLA (CANDIDATE A): Yes, you must bring scissors and a pencil.
SERGEJ (CANDIDATE B): And do you know where the lessons are?
ELLA (CANDIDATE A): Yes, in class room 251. That's on the second floor.
SERGEJ (CANDIDATE B): Thank you very much, Ella.
ELLA (CANDIDATE A): You're welcome.

PRÜFER/IN: Sergej, here is some information about **jobs at Hotel Breezy Lake**. Ella, you don't know anything about the job, so ask Sergej some questions about it. Now Ella, ask Sergej your questions and Sergej you answer them.
ELLA (CANDIDATE A): Sergej, do you know where the job is?

SERGEJ (CANDIDATE B): It's at the Breezy Lake Hotel.
ELLA (CANDIDATE A): And can you tell me what (sort of) job this is?
SERGEJ (CANDIDATE B): They need help in the kitchen. It's a job for students.
ELLA (CANDIDATE A): How much do they pay?
SERGEJ (CANDIDATE B): You will get 7 pounds per hour.
ELLA (CANDIDATE A): What are the working hours? (When will I have to work?)
SERGEJ (CANDIDATE B): Friday to Sunday from five to nine in the evening.
ELLA (CANDIDATE A): Have you got a contact number?
SERGEJ (CANDIDATE B): Yes, it's 271 472 (you can also write an email).
ELLA (CANDIDATE A): Thanks a lot.
SERGEJ (CANDIDATE B): Not at all.

Sprachenzertifikat Englisch A2
Mock Exam 2

Paper 1: Reading and Writing

Part 1

Questions 1–5
*Which notice (**A–H**) says this (**1–5**)?*
*For questions 1–5, mark the correct letters **A–H** on your answer sheet.*

Example:

0. There are no dancing classes at the moment. **F**

1. Call this person if you would like special entertainment for your party. ☐
2. Parents will get their children's presents in time for Christmas. ☐
3. Talk to this person if you want a job. ☐
4. If you buy this you get more entertainment without paying extra. ☐
5. Contact this person if you want someone to look after your children. ☐

A Trains are not running this weekend because of strike

B The DVD collection includes 3 new episodes free of charge

C all toys will be delivered in November at the latest

D SALE! 30 % off all boots & winter shoes this week

E Chris the Clown comes to your home: call 9385032 for more information

F Ballet lessons start again next month (November)

G Cleaners wanted for office building (2 evenings and Saturday 7 – 10 am) apply within, ask for Mr Benson

H Do you need help at home? Granny Maud is a good cook and loves children. Call 0934 - 845834 after 3 pm

Part 2

Questions 6–10
Read the sentences about a girl working in a pet shop.
*Choose the best word (**A, B** or **C**) for each space.*
*For questions 6–10, mark **A**, **B** or **C** on your answer sheet.*

Example:

0. Emily loves … with animals.

   A ☐ selling **B** ☐ interesting **C** ☑ working

6. Rabbits are Emily's … animals.

   A ☐ loving **B** ☐ favourite **C** ☐ liked

7. In the morning she … all the cages and feeds the pets.

   A ☐ changes **B** ☐ cleans **C** ☐ brush

8. Emily would like to open her own pet shop when she has … enough money.

   A ☐ spared **B** ☐ bought **C** ☐ saved

9. Her boss, Mrs Singer, thinks Emily is a very good …

   A ☐ shop assistant **B** ☐ help **C** ☐ pet shopper

10. The people who come to the shop like Emily because she is very friendly and knows … about all the pets there.

    A ☐ a lot of **B** ☐ many **C** ☐ a lot

Part 3

Questions 11–15
Complete the five conversations.
*For questions 11–15, mark **A**, **B** or **C** on your answer sheet.*

Example:

0. Did you understand what the teacher said?

   A ☐ Nothing special.
   B ☑ Not really.
   C ☐ It's not enough.

11. I hope Henry will be here soon.

    A ☐ Don't mention it.
    B ☐ Don't worry, he will.
    C ☐ Doesn't he?

12. What would you like?
- **A** ☐ I'll have a cup of tea and a biscuit, please.
- **B** ☐ I like tea with milk.
- **C** ☐ I prefer coffee.

13. And what do I do when this light goes on?
- **A** ☐ He presses the button.
- **B** ☐ No, you can't do it.
- **C** ☐ Just push the red button.

14. What car will you buy?
- **A** ☐ This one is new.
- **B** ☐ It's very interesting.
- **C** ☐ I haven't decided yet.

15. Can I show you some shirts?
- **A** ☐ Oh yes, please.
- **B** ☐ Yes, I like them.
- **C** ☐ No, I don't like it.

Questions 16–20
Complete the conversation between a teacher and his student.
What does Mr Henson say to Tim?
*For questions 16–20, mark the correct letter **A–H** on your answer sheet.*

Example:

Mr Henson: Hello Tim. Are you in form A5 this year?

Tim: **0.** E

Mr Henson: Do you have classes in the afternoon?

Tim: **16.** ______

Mr Henson: That's good to hear because we are still looking for people to join our computer club on Wednesday afternoon. I think you like computers a lot, don't you?

Tim: **17.** ______

Mr Henson: Well, then just come to the computer room on the second floor next Wednesday at two o'clock. Mrs Hunter will be there to help you.

Tim: **18.** ______

A Yes, that's right and I'd like to learn more about graphic design, too.

B Yes, but only on Tuesday and Thursday.

C It's quite difficult anyway.

D There are some students in my class who haven't got their books yet.

E No, I'm in B5 together with Mark and Sue.

F Great, I'm really looking forward to it.

Mr Henson: Oh, and can you tell your classmates to bring their English workbooks? We are starting a new lesson tomorrow.

Tim: **19.** ______

Mr Henson: Hm. Can you go and see Harry at the library to make sure they get their books as soon as possible?

Oliver: **20.** ______

Mr Henson: OK, great. See you tomorrow.

G OK, I'll talk to him right after break.

H Yes, that's fine and there are lots of books.

Part 4

Questions 21–27
Read the text about Robert, who works in a travel agency.
*Are the sentences 21–27 'Right' (**A**) or 'Wrong' (**B**)?*
*If there is not enough information to answer 'Right' (**A**) or 'Wrong' (**B**), choose 'Doesn't say' (**C**).*
*For questions 21–27, mark **A**, **B** or **C** on your answer sheet.*

Robert Harper

Robert Harper works in a large travel agency in Scotland. He likes his job very much although he usually has a lot of work to do.

"The best thing about working here is that I can travel all over the world in my free time. And often I get good prices, too. Hotel staff are very friendly because they hope that I'll recommend their hotel to my customers. It is really true that you can sell something better if you have seen it yourself. You hear about all the interesting places and new hotels and resorts. As we are a very big company, we have partners around the globe. Sometimes we also travel to nice places during our work. Most people think this is wonderful but it can be stressful, too. Imagine being a nice holiday island and instead of relaxing on the beach you have to visit 10 hotels per day.

In my daily work at the office I like talking to our customers and trying to find the perfect holiday for them. We also get a lot of calls from business people who book flights or rental cars. Sometimes it is really difficult to find what they want and they often have to change their plans. I like working on the computer but one disadvantage of my job is all the paperwork I have to do."

Example:

0. Robert Harper works in a travel agency.

A ☑ Right **B** ☐ Wrong **C** ☐ Doesn't say

21. Robert works in the USA.
A ☐ Right **B** ☐ Wrong **C** ☐ Doesn't say

22. He often travels with his family when he visits new hotels.
A ☐ Right **B** ☐ Wrong **C** ☐ Doesn't say

23. Hotel staff are very unfriendly to people who work in travel agencies.
A ☐ Right **B** ☐ Wrong **C** ☐ Doesn't say

24. Robert sometimes travels during his work.
A ☐ Right **B** ☐ Wrong **C** ☐ Doesn't say

25. Robert also has to visit a lot of restaurants when he travels to visit new places.
A ☐ Right **B** ☐ Wrong **C** ☐ Doesn't say

26. It is not always easy to book flights for business people.
A ☐ Right **B** ☐ Wrong **C** ☐ Doesn't say

27. Robert likes doing paperwork.
A ☐ Right **B** ☐ Wrong **C** ☐ Doesn't say

Part 5

Questions 28–35
*Read the article about curry. Choose the best answer (**A**, **B** or **C**) for each space.*
*For answers 28–35, mark **A**, **B** or **C** on your answer sheet.*

Curry

When we hear curry (0) ___we___ usually think of a yellow spicy powder. A typical Indian curry powder consists (28) __________ many different spices.

Most families have (29) __________ own recipes. They use more (30) __________ 15 different ingredients. The mixtures (31) __________ called Masalas and can have a mild (32) __________ very spicy taste. The yellow colour comes (33) __________ a root (34) __________ is called Curcuma and is used in nearly every curry powder. Originally the word curry was used for the many spicy meals the British people brought back from their colonies (35) __________ the 19th century.

Example:

	A		B		C	
0.	A	☐ he	B	☑ we	C	☐ one
28.	A	☐ from	B	☐ over	C	☐ of
29.	A	☐ an	B	☐ their	C	☐ they
30.	A	☐ them	B	☐ than	C	☐ then
31.	A	☐ are	B	☐ some	C	☐ is
32.	A	☐ of	B	☐ or	C	☐ from
33.	A	☐ from	B	☐ by	C	☐ over
34.	A	☐ this	B	☐ who	C	☐ which
35.	A	☐ at	B	☐ in	C	☐ by

Part 6

Questions 36–40
Read the descriptions of some things you can see in a kitchen.
What is the word for each one?
The first letter is already there. There is one space for each other letter in the word.
For questions 36–40, write the words on your answer sheet.

Example:

0. You drink juice from a … g l a s s.

36. You need this to cut your food. k _ _ _ _

37. Cakes and roasts are baked or cooked in the o _ _ _.

38. The place where butter and milk are stored to keep them cool. f _ _ _ _ _

39. You eat your food from a p _ _ _ _.

40. Sausages and steaks are fried in a p _ _.

Part 7

Questions 41–50
Complete the information Harriet wrote about her club.
*Write **one** word for each space.*
For questions 41–50, write the words on your answer sheet.

Example: (0) *name*

Hello,

My (**0**) __name__ is Harriet Summers and I (**41**) __________ in Birmingham. I have started a cooking club together with (**42**) __________ sister Julia. After 6 months the club has already got 14 (**43**) __________. We meet every Wednesday (**44**) __________ 4 pm. First, we do some shopping and (**45**) __________ all the things we need. Then we go to our school kitchen and prepare the meal. At the moment there are 9 girls and 5 (**46**) __________. Cooking usually (**47**) __________ about one hour and is real fun. However, the best part is (**48**) __________ we sit down and eat together. Of course, we (**49**) __________ to clean the kitchen afterwards, but it is easy with so many helpers. If you are interested (**50**) __________ joining our club, just send me an email to harrisum@xyz.co.uk.

Part 8

Questions 51–55
Read the information and the note Pia wrote.
Fill in the information on the form.
For questions 51–55, write the information on your answer sheet.

NEW WATER BALLET LESSONS FOR GIRLS!

EVERY TUESDAY 3 PM - 4.30 PM (9-12 YEARS)
EVERY THURSDAY 4 PM - 5.30 PM (13-16 YEARS)
OR FRIDAY 4 PM - 5.30 PM (13-16 YEARS)

PER MONTH 35.00 EUROS, MEMBERS OF THE SWIM CLUB PAY ONLY 25.00 EUROS. YOU WILL ALSO NEED A RED SWIMSUIT. WE ORDER THE SUITS AT A SPECIAL PRICE. TICK THE BOX AND WE WILL TALK ABOUT SIZES LATER.

IF YOU ARE INTERESTED, FILL IN A FORM AND RETURN IT BY FRIDAY, 27TH MARCH.

PAULINA HALL

Mum,
Could you please fill in the form for me und give it to Paulina when you go swimming tonight?
Don't forget that I'll be 13 next week and that I am a member of the swim club. I will need a new red swimsuit as mine is green and very old!
I can start in May and don't forget that I have lessons on Thursday afternoon until 5pm.
Thanks and see you at 8,
Pia

WATER BALLET REGISTRATION FORM

Name:		Pia Conolly
Age next week:	**51**	
Day of the week:	**52**	
Starting in (month):	**53**	
Swimsuit needed?	**54**	☐ yes ☐ no
Cost:	**55**	€ ______

Part 9

Question 56
You are on holiday with your parents. Write a postcard to your friend Phil.

Say:
- where you are on holiday
- what you can do there
- how long you are staying

Write 25–35 words.
Write the postcard on your answer sheet.

Paper 2: Listening

Tracks 10–14

Part 1

You will hear five short conversations.
You will hear each conversation twice.
There is one question for each conversation.
For questions 1–5, put a tick (✓) under the right answer.

Example:

0. When did the concert start?

   WOMAN: Did the concert start at three o'clock yesterday?

   MAN: No, they had planned to start at three thirty but the bus was late so they started at four.

A ☐

B ☐

C ☑

1. Where are the woman's keys?

A ☐

B ☐

C ☐

2. Which chocolates does Oliver buy?

A ☐

B ☐

C ☐

3. Where does Martin work?

A ☐

B ☐

C ☐

4. How are they travelling to London?

A ☐

B ☐

C ☐

5. How did the family spend their holiday?

A ☐

B ☐

C ☐

Part 2

Track 15

Questions 6–10
Listen to Elisa telling her teacher about the schedule for a celebration at their school next Saturday.
What are they doing at each time?
*For questions 6–10, write a letter (**A–H**) next to each time.*
You will hear the conversation twice.

Example:

0. 9 o'clock	C		**A**	Prepare class rooms
6. 10 o'clock	☐		**B**	Headmaster's opening speech
7. 11 o'clock	☐		**C**	Prepare buffet
8. 2 o'clock	☐		**D**	Opening of buffet
9. 3 o'clock	☐		**E**	Football match
10. 5 o'clock	☐		**F**	Welcome former students
			G	Play
			H	Press conference

Part 3

Track 16

Questions 11–15
Listen to Roberta and Thomas talking about a new restaurant.
*For questions 11–15, tick (✓) **A**, **B** or **C**.*
You will hear the conversation twice.

Example:

0. The name of the restaurant is
   - **A** ☐ El Pizza.
   - **B** ☑ La Piazza.
   - **C** ☐ La Plaza.

11. How did Roberta find out about the restaurant?
   - **A** ☐ Advert in the local newspaper
   - **B** ☐ Posters
   - **C** ☐ Radio

12. What did Thomas' grandfather eat?
   - **A** ☐ Salad
   - **B** ☐ Pizza
   - **C** ☐ Pasta

13. What do Thomas and his parents not do on Fridays?
    - **A** ☐ Go swimming
    - **B** ☐ Go shopping
    - **C** ☐ Go to the library

14. When does Roberta's piano lesson end on Fridays?
    - **A** ☐ 4 pm
    - **B** ☐ 3 pm
    - **C** ☐ 6 pm

15. Who is coming to the restaurant with Roberta?
    - **A** ☐ Her brother
    - **B** ☐ Her class mate
    - **C** ☐ Her sister

Part 4

Track 17

Questions 16–20
You will hear a conversation about a bus trip.
Listen and complete questions 16–20.
You will hear the conversation twice.

BUS TRIP TO BARCELONA		
Passenger's name:		Sandra HELLER
Travels from:	**16**	______________
Number of nights:	**17**	______________
Price:	**18**	€ ______________
Departure/Travel Date:	**19**	______________
Pays by:	**20**	______________

Part 5

Track 18 *Questions 21–25*
You will hear a recorded message.
Listen and complete questions 21–25.
You will hear the information twice.

FLOOPSIE INFO LINE		
On Fridays the plays start at:	**21**	______________
"The Robber Hotzenplotz" is on in:	**22**	______________
Family ticket price:	**23**	£ ______________
Cafeteria offers coffee, soft drinks and	**24**	______________ of the plays
Booking Hotline (9 am – 3 pm):	**25**	Monday – ______________

You now have 8 minutes to write your answers on the answer sheet.

Paper 3: Speaking

Part 1

Part 1 consists of a short conversation with the examiner. You should be familiar with the language associated with meeting people for the first time and you should be able to give information of a personal kind, e. g name, place of origin, occupation, family etc. You are also expected to talk about your daily life, your hobbies etc.

Part 2

Prompt cards are used to stimulate questions and answers. The examiner gives instructions and hands out a question card to one candidate and an answer card to the other. After the candidates have asked and answered their questions, they change roles.

Example

The examiner gives a question card to Candidate B and an answer card to Candidate A.

Candidate A, here is some information about Hot Air Balloon Trips.

Candidate B, you don't know anything about such trips, so ask A some questions about it. Now B, ask A your questions about the trips and A, you answer them.

Candidate A – your information.

Every weekend

€75 per person

Call 4584574 for tickets

Special prices for families

Great for company outings!

Candidate B – your questions.

Hot Air Balloon Trips

- Where?
- When?
- Cost?
- Buy tickets?
- Discount?

Candidate B, here is some information about snow shoes.

Candidate A, you don't know anything about such snow shoes, so ask B some questions about these lessons. Now A, ask B your questions about the shoes and B, you answer them.

Candidate B – your information.

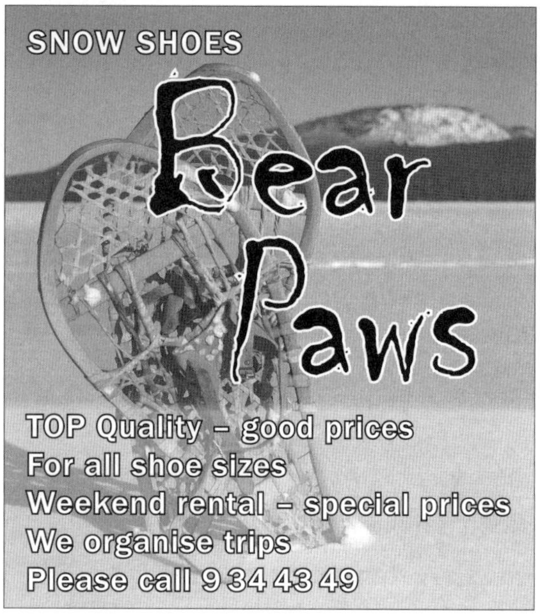

Candidate A – your questions.

Snow Shoes

- Name?
- Good/price?
- Size?
- Must buy?
- Trips?

Lösungsvorschläge

Reading and Writing

Part 1

1. Call this person if you would like special entertainment for your party. **E**
2. Parents will get their children's presents in time for Christmas. **C**
3. Talk to this person if you want a job. **G**
4. If you buy this you get more entertainment without paying extra. **B**
5. Contact this person if you want someone to look after your children. **H**

Part 2

6. Rabbits are Emily's … animals.
   A ☐ loving **B** ☑ favourite **C** ☐ liked

7. In the morning she … all the cages and feeds the pets.
   A ☐ changes **B** ☑ cleans **C** ☐ brush

8. Emily would like to open her own pet shop when she has … enough money.
   A ☐ spared **B** ☐ bought **C** ☑ saved

9. Her boss, Mrs Singer, thinks Emily is a very good …
   A ☑ shop assistant **B** ☐ help **C** ☐ pet shopper

10. The people who come to the shop like Emily because she is very friendly and knows … about all the pets there.
    A ☐ a lot of **B** ☐ many **C** ☑ a lot

Part 3

11. I hope Henry will be here soon.
    A ☐ Don't mention it.
    B ☑ Don't worry, he will.
    C ☐ Doesn't he?

12. What would you like?
- A ☑ I'll have a cup of tea and a biscuit, please.
- B ☐ I like tea with milk.
- C ☐ I prefer coffee.

13. And what do I do when this light goes on?
- A ☐ He presses the button.
- B ☐ No, you can't do it.
- C ☑ Just push the red button.

14. What car will you buy?
- A ☐ This one is new.
- B ☐ It's very interesting.
- C ☑ I haven't decided yet.

15. Can I show you some shirts?
- A ☑ Oh yes, please.
- B ☐ Yes, I like them.
- C ☐ No, I don't like it.

Mr Henson: Do you have classes in the afternoon?

Tim: 16. B

Mr Henson: That's good to hear because we are still looking for people to join our computer club on Wednesday afternoon. I think you like computers a lot, don't you?

Tim: 17. A

Mr Henson: Well, then just come to the computer room on the second floor next Wednesday at two o'clock. Mrs Hunter will be there to help you.

Tim: 18. F

Mr Henson: Oh, and can you tell your classmates to bring their English workbooks? We are starting a new lesson tomorrow.

Tim: 19. D

Mr Henson: Hm. Can you go and see Harry at the library to make sure they get their books as soon as possible?

Oliver: 20. G

Mr Henson: OK, great. See you tomorrow.

Part 4

21. Robert works in the USA.

A ☐ Right **B** ☑ Wrong **C** ☐ Doesn't say

22. He often travels with his family when he visits new hotels.

A ☐ Right **B** ☐ Wrong **C** ☑ Doesn't say

23. Hotel staff are very unfriendly to people who work in travel agencies.

A ☐ Right **B** ☑ Wrong **C** ☐ Doesn't say

24. Robert sometimes travels during his work.

A ☑ Right **B** ☐ Wrong **C** ☐ Doesn't say

25. Robert also has to visit a lot of restaurants when he travels to visit new places.

A ☐ Right **B** ☐ Wrong **C** ☑ Doesn't say

26. It is not always easy to book flights for business people.

A ☑ Right **B** ☐ Wrong **C** ☐ Doesn't say

27. Robert likes doing paperwork.

A ☐ Right **B** ☑ Wrong **C** ☐ Doesn't say

Part 5

28. **A** ☐ from **B** ☐ over **C** ☑ of

29. **A** ☐ an **B** ☑ their **C** ☐ they

30. **A** ☐ them **B** ☑ than **C** ☐ then

31. **A** ☑ are **B** ☐ some **C** ☐ is

32. **A** ☐ of **B** ☑ or **C** ☐ from

33. **A** ☑ from **B** ☐ by **C** ☐ over

34. **A** ☐ this **B** ☐ who **C** ☑ which

35. **A** ☐ at **B** ☑ in **C** ☐ by

Part 6

36. You need this to cut your food. **knife**

37. Cakes and roasts are baked or cooked in the **oven**.

38. The place where butter and milk are stored to keep them cool. **fridge**

39. You eat your food from a **plate**.

40. Sausages and steaks are fried in a **pan**.

Part 7

Hello,
My (**0**) **name** is Harriet Summers and I (**41**) **live** in Birmingham. I have started a cooking club together with (**42**) **my** sister Julia. After 6 months the club has already got 14 (**43**) **members**. We meet every Wednesday (**44**) **at** 4 pm. First, we do some shopping and (**45**) **buy/get** all the things we need. Then we go to our school kitchen and prepare the meal. At the moment there are 9 girls and 5 (**46**) **boys**. Cooking usually (**47**) **takes** about one hour and is real fun. However, the best part is (**48**) **when** we sit down and eat together. Of course, we (**49**) **have** to clean the kitchen afterwards, but it is easy with so many helpers. If you are interested (**50**) **in** joining our club, just send me an email to harrisum@xyz.co.uk.

Part 8

Age next week:	**51**	*13*
Day of the week:	**52**	*Friday*
Starting in (month):	**53**	*May*
Swimsuit needed?	**54**	☑ yes ☐ no
Cost:	**55**	*€ 25.00*

Part 9

Dear Phil,
I am on holiday in Sweden with my parents. It's great here, we go swimming every day in a lake and ride our bikes. We are going to stay for another week.
See you soon,
Helga

Listening

Part 1

Tracks 10–14

1. **Where are the woman's keys?**
   Woman: I can't find my keys. I thought they were on the table.
   Man: Didn't you put them in your handbag this morning?
   Woman: Yes, I did. Ah, now I remember. I left them in the car!

2. **Which chocolates does Oliver buy?**
   Man: I need a box of chocolates for my aunt Sue. I think I'll take vanilla toffees.
   Woman: Why don't you take strawberry? Aunt Sue loves strawberries.
   Man: Or hazelnut? But I think you're right, fruit's nicer in the summer.

3. **Where does Martin work?**
   Woman: Do you know where Martin works?
   Man: Well, first he went to Spain and worked in a factory there.
   Woman: Yes, I know but I thought he became a teacher then.
   Man: I don't know. The last two years he's been working in a hospital and his sister says he really likes the job.

4. **How are they travelling to London?**
   Man: Shall we take the bus to London?
   Woman: Why don't we go by train?
   Man: Haven't you heard that there's a strike?
   Woman: Oh no, not again. We'll have to go by bus anyway then.
   Man: We could take a taxi. It's not that far.
   Woman: Yes, but it's still quite expensive.
   Man: Alright then, do you think we can catch the 12.15?

5. **How did the family spend their holiday?**
   Boy: What did you do in the summer holidays?
   Girl: We wanted to go climbing but Mum said it was too dangerous.
   Boy: So what did you do then?
   Girl: Dad wanted to relax on a beach but in the end we decided to spend our holidays on a farm. We had a great time, I went horse riding every day! Dad still found a quiet lake to swim in and relax, so everyone was happy.

1. Where are the woman's keys?

A ☐ **B** ☑ **C** ☐

2. Which chocolates does Oliver buy?

A ☐ **B** ☐ **C** ☑

3. Where does Martin work?

A ☐ **B** ☐ **C** ☑

4. How are they travelling to London?

A ☑ B ☐ C ☐

5. How did the family spend their holiday?

A ☐ B ☑ C ☐

Part 2

Track 15

TEACHER: OK, Elisa have you and your team finished the plans for our celebration this Saturday?

ELISA: Yes, we have. We'll meet in the hall at 9 o'clock and prepare all the cakes and the food for the buffet.

TEACHER: OK, what's next?

ELISA: Mr Robson, the headmaster, will make his opening speech at 10 o'clock.

TEACHER: OK, by then the press and most of the parents will have arrived.

ELISA: The speech will last about 20 minutes, and then we'll have time to show the parents round.

TEACHER: Right, and at 11 I will officially open the buffet. Then everyone can walk round and look at all the stands and exhibitions.

ELISA: Yes, exactly. The next official part is at 2 in the afternoon when we welcome some of our former students. The press are going to take some photos then.

TEACHER: OK. By the way, have you spoken to Ken Holler?

ELISA: Yes, he sends his regards! He said he wanted to play against your team in the football match at 3.

TEACHER: That sounds like him! OK, so we'll have the football match at three then.

ELISA: Yes, and the last official part is the play at 5 o'clock. The students have prepared everything and there's going to be a dress rehearsal tonight.
TEACHER: OK, fine, you've done a good job!
ELISA: Thank you. I'm really looking forward to Saturday.

6. 10 o'clock **B**
7. 11 o'clock **D**
8. 2 o'clock **F**
9. 3 o'clock **E**
10. 5 o'clock **G**

Part 3

Track 16

ROBERTA: Hi Thomas. Have you been to the new restaurant in the city centre?
THOMAS: The Italian place?
ROBERTA: Yes, "La Piazza".
THOMAS: Yes, I went there with my granddad and his colleagues last Saturday.
ROBERTA: What do you think of it? I saw their posters everywhere.
THOMAS: Yeah, they put an advert in the local newspaper, too. Well, the food is absolutely delicious.
ROBERTA: What did you have?
THOMAS: I had a pizza and my granddad had pasta. They also serve nice salads.
ROBERTA: Wow, I have to go there.
THOMAS: Why don't you come with me and my parents? We go swimming on Friday and then to the library. Afterwards we're always very hungry.
ROBERTA: I'd love to, but I have piano lessons on Fridays until 4 o'clock and then I go shopping for Mrs Benson.
THOMAS: Never mind. We won't get to "La Piazza" until 6.30.
ROBERTA: OK, then. Do you think I could bring my sister Pat as well?
THOMAS: Yes, of course. My dad's colleague and his son are also coming with us.

11. How did Roberta find out about the restaurant?
    - **A** ☐ Advert in the local newspaper
    - **B** ☑ Posters
    - **C** ☐ Radio

12. What did Thomas' grandfather eat?
    - **A** ☐ Salad
    - **B** ☐ Pizza
    - **C** ☑ Pasta

13. What do Thomas and his parents not do on Fridays?
   A ☐ Go swimming
   B ☑ Go shopping
   C ☐ Go to the library

14. When does Roberta's piano lesson end on Fridays?
   A ☑ 4 pm
   B ☐ 3 pm
   C ☐ 6 pm

15. Who is coming to the restaurant with Roberta?
   A ☐ Her brother
   B ☐ Her class mate
   C ☑ Her sister

Part 4

Track 17

MAN: Good morning. Transeurope Bus Services.

WOMAN: Good morning, I'd like some information about your bus trips to Barcelona, please. Where do the buses leave from?

MAN: You can travel from Frankfurt, Berlin and Munich.

WOMAN: Munich would be best for me. Could you give me some more details, please?

MAN: Of course. We start from Munich at 5 pm on Friday and arrive in Barcelona the next afternoon. You can stay for 3 or 4 nights.

WOMAN: I think I'd prefer 4 nights.

MAN: So, for 4 nights including breakfast it is 425 euros in a 4-star hotel. You could also stay in a 3-star hotel for 380.

WOMAN: I'll take the 3-star hotel. Or no, I don't travel that often, make it the 4-star hotel, please.

MAN: Alright, and when would you like to travel?

WOMAN: Well, if possible next Friday, the 17th.

MAN: You're lucky, we have three seats left. Can I take your name please?

WOMAN: Sandra Heller. That's H – E – L – L – E – R.

MAN: OK, and how would you like to pay, Ms Heller? By credit card or bank transfer?

WOMAN: Credit card, please, but I haven't got the card with me right now. I'll call you again this afternoon.

MAN: OK, thank you. Goodbye for now.

WOMAN: Thank you. Speak to you later.

Travels from:	16	Munich
Number of nights:	17	4
Price:	18	€ 425.00
Departure/Travel Date:	19	Friday, 17th
Pays by:	20	Credit card

Part 5

Track 18

Good afternoon, this is the FLOOPSIE puppet theatre information line. Our plays start at 4.30 on Friday and at 10 am and 3 pm on Saturdays and Sundays. In March we are playing “the Robber Hotzenplotz” and in April and May “ Pippi Longstocking”. The plays are suitable for children between 4 and 10. Tickets are £4 on Fridays and £5 on Saturdays and Sundays. Please note that the price for the family ticket is now £15 and not £12 as it was last year and still may be printed in some of our brochures. It is recommended to book seats in advance, especially for groups of more than 6 people. During the break you can buy soft drinks, coffee and posters of all our plays from the cafeteria. You can bring your own food or get sandwiches and cakes from the baker’s in our basement. For further information and ticket reservation please call 475391, Monday to Thursday from 9 am to 3 pm.

On Fridays the plays start at:	21	4.30
“The Robber Hotzenplotz” is on in:	22	March
Family ticket price:	23	£ 15
Cafeteria offers coffee, soft drinks and	24	posters of the plays
Booking Hotline (9 am – 3 pm):	25	Monday – Thursday

Speaking

Part 2

ELLA (CANDIDATE B): (I'd like some information on hot-air balloon trips.) Can you tell me where I can go on a **hot-air balloon trip**?
STEFAN (CANDIDATE A): In the Bavarian Forest. They say it's great for company outings.
ELLA (CANDIDATE B): And when can I go?
STEFAN (CANDIDATE A): You can go every weekend.
ELLA (CANDIDATE B): How much is a trip (in a hot-air balloon)?
STEFAN (CANDIDATE A): It's 75 Euros per person.
ELLA (CANDIDATE B): Where can I get tickets?
STEFAN (CANDIDATE A): There is a telephone number for reservations, it's 458 45 74. (You can call 458 45 74 to buy a ticket.)
ELLA (CANDIDATE B): Is there a discount?
STEFAN (CANDIDATE A): Yes, they offer special prices for families. (Yes, families get a special price.)

STEFAN (CANDIDATE A): Can you give me some information about the **snow shoes**?
ELLA (CANDIDATE B): Yes, of course, what would you like to know?
STEFAN (CANDIDATE A): What's the name of the snow shoe company?
ELLA (CANDIDATE B): They are called Bear Paws.
STEFAN (CANDIDATE A): Are they good quality? Do you know anything about the price? (How much are they?)
ELLA (CANDIDATE B): It says they are top quality at a very good price. (I don't have an exact price but they say the quality is top.)
STEFAN (CANDIDATE A): What (shoe) sizes are available? (Do you know anything about the sizes?)
ELLA (CANDIDATE B): They fit all sizes.
STEFAN (CANDIDATE A): Do you have to buy the snow shoes?
ELLA (CANDIDATE B): No, you can also rent them. (No, there are special prices for weekend rental.)
STEFAN (CANDIDATE A): Can I go in a group? (Is it good for groups?)
ELLA (CANDIDATE B): Yes, they organise group trips.
STEFAN (CANDIDATE A): Ok, thank you very much.
ELLA (CANDIDATE B): Not at all.

Sprachenzertifikat Englisch A2
Mock Exam 3

Paper 1: Reading and Writing

Part 1

Questions 1–5
*Which notice (**A–H**) says this (**1–5**)?*
*For questions 1–5, mark the correct letters **A–H** on your answer sheet.*

Example:

0. You cannot borrow any books this week. **D**

1. To get a reduced price you must go here at a special time. ☐
2. Go here if you need your clothes cleaned quickly. ☐
3. You cannot go here every day. ☐
4. If you want to make a phone call, you have to go outside. ☐
5. You must pay cash for this service. ☐

A No mobile phones inside the museum please

B **repair work (9 – 11 am)** please use lift next door

C Restaurant Delhi Palace
half-price meals at lunchtime (11 am – 1 pm)

D **FLOODING**
Library closed this week

E **Have coins ready – this public phone does not accept cards**

F Dry Cleaners – express service

G Ben's ice-cream 4 new flavours NEW! diet ice-cream

H Visit our show-room on 2nd floor
open daily 9 am – 3 pm except Sundays

Part 2

Questions 6–10
Read the sentences about Mr Walters and his hobby.
*Choose the best word (**A, B** or **C**) for each space.*
*For questions 6–10, mark **A**, **B** or **C** on your answer sheet.*

Example:

0. Mr Walters loves … with his model trains.
   A ☐ building **B** ☐ driving **C** ☑ playing

6. Each Saturday after … he meets his friends from the model railway club.
   A ☐ launch **B** ☐ lounge **C** ☐ lunch

7. His hobby is quite … but Mr Walters also builds a lot himself to save money.
   A ☐ cheap **B** ☐ valuable **C** ☐ expensive

8. His family give him a new locomotive as a Christmas … each year.
   A ☐ packet **B** ☐ present **C** ☐ package

9. Over the … he has built a huge model railway in the basement of his house.
   A ☐ years **B** ☐ times **C** ☐ ages

10. Next month Mr Walters wants to make a … to the railway museum with his friends.
   A ☐ travel **B** ☐ trip **C** ☐ voyage

Part 3

Questions 11–15
Complete the five conversations.
*For questions 11–15, mark **A**, **B** or **C** on your answer sheet.*

Example:

0. Did you understand what the teacher said?
   A ☐ Nothing special.
   B ☑ Not really.
   C ☐ It's not enough.

11. Can I go now?
   A ☐ After 2.30 pm.
   B ☐ No, I'll go there.
   C ☐ Yes, sure.

12. Where are you going this summer?
A ☐ Let's go then.
B ☐ We haven't decided yet.
C ☐ I prefer Spain.

13. How long are you going to stay in Brazil?
A ☐ For at least two weeks.
B ☐ The last two weeks.
C ☐ In two weeks.

14. Which pen is yours?
A ☐ This one is new.
B ☐ It doesn't matter.
C ☐ The blue one.

15. Say hello to Alison when you see her!
A ☐ Hello there.
B ☐ Yes, I like her.
C ☐ I will.

Questions 16–20
Complete the conversation between two friends.
What does Robin say to Nina?
*For questions 16–20, mark the correct letter **A–H** on your answer sheet.*

Example:

Robin: Hello Nina. How are you?

Nina: **0.** B

Robin: I'm fine, but I have to finish this report. I want to see the Polar Stars' ice-hockey match tonight.

Nina: **16.** ______

Robin: Yes, my sister gave it to me as a birthday present. I'm a big fan of the Polar Stars.

Nina: **17.** ______

Robin: Yes, and they have won the cup three times now. Why don't you come, too?

Nina **18.** ______

Robin: Oh yes, during the week they usually have some tickets left. The weekend matches are always sold out, though.

Nina: **19.** ______

Robin: At 5 pm. Why don't we meet at the ice-rink at 4 o'clock? We can get a ticket for you and meet my friends there.

Nina: **20.** ______

Robin: Well, see you later then.

A OK, that sounds great. I'll be there.

B Fine, thanks. And you?

C Do you think I can get a ticket?

D I don't think they'll win.

E When does the match start?

F Who's your favourite player?

G Wow, have you got a ticket?

H So am I. They really have the best players.

Part 4

Questions 21–27
Read the text about Lady Godiva.
*Are the sentences 21–27 'Right' (**A**) or 'Wrong' (**B**)?*
*If there is not enough information to answer 'Right' (**A**) or 'Wrong' (**B**), choose 'Doesn't say' (**C**).*
*For questions 21–27, mark **A**, **B** or **C** on your answer sheet.*

Lady Godiva

Most people in England know the story of Lady Godiva. She lived in the 11th century and was the wife of a very powerful nobleman. His name was Leofric, Earl of Mercia, and he took very high taxes from his people. Lady Godiva was a kind-hearted woman. She knew that the poor people could not pay the money and wanted to help them.

One day Lady Godiva asked her husband if she could do anything to lower the taxes for the people of Coventry. The Earl said he would not take money from the people anymore if Lady Godiva rode naked through the streets on a horse. Of course, he thought she would never do this.

Lady Godiva decided to take her husband at his word. She sent messengers round who told everyone to stay in their houses and keep doors and windows shut. Then she sat naked on a horse and wrapped her long hair around herself. She rode through Coventry and the people stayed inside their homes as they had promised. Nobody was out in the streets and only one man tried to look at Lady Godiva as she rode by. His name was Tom and the legend goes that he turned blind immediately. The Earl, however, did as he had promised and never took taxes from his people again.

Example:

0. Lady Godiva lived in France in the 11th century.

A ☐ Right **B** ☑ Wrong **C** ☐ Doesn't say

21. Lady Godiva did not want to help the poor people.

A ☐ Right **B** ☐ Wrong **C** ☐ Doesn't say

22. The Earl did not think Lady Godiva would ride naked through the town.

A ☐ Right **B** ☐ Wrong **C** ☐ Doesn't say

23. Some ladies helped Lady Godiva to comb her hair.

A ☐ Right **B** ☐ Wrong **C** ☐ Doesn't say

24. Lady Godiva sent messengers round to tell the people what to do.

A ☐ Right **B** ☐ Wrong **C** ☐ Doesn't say

25. Some people tried to watch her ride through Coventry.

A ☐ Right **B** ☐ Wrong **C** ☐ Doesn't say

26. It took her four hours to ride through the town.

A ☐ Right **B** ☐ Wrong **C** ☐ Doesn't say

27. After her ride the people of Coventry no longer had to pay taxes to Earl Leofric.

A ☐ Right **B** ☐ Wrong **C** ☐ Doesn't say

Part 5

Questions 28–35
*Read the article about the king penguins. Choose the best answer (**A**, **B** or **C**) for each space.*
*For answers 28–35, mark **A**, **B** or **C** on your answer sheet.*

KING PENGUINS

Did you know (0) ___that___ King Penguins do not breed their eggs in nests? They carry them around on (28) __________ feet. The female penguin lays one egg which (29) __________ then kept warm by (30) __________ birds in turns. The penguins even tear out their own feathers (31) __________ keep the egg warm and close to the body. It takes around 55 days (32) __________ the little penguin hatches from the egg. The partner who is not breeding (33) __________ to get all the food during this time. Even after the chick is hatched from the egg the parents keep it warm and sheltered in the pouch. The little penguin would not be (34) __________ to survive and has to stay with its parents for at (35) __________ another month.

Example:

0. **A** ☐ while **B** ☑ that **C** ☐ for

28. **A** ☐ his **B** ☐ them **C** ☐ their

29. **A** ☐ is **B** ☐ was **C** ☐ were

30. **A**	☐ a	**B**	☐ both	**C**	☐ them
31. **A**	☐ for	**B**	☐ to	**C**	☐ as
32. **A**	☐ until	**B**	☐ by	**C**	☐ from
33. **A**	☐ must	**B**	☐ have	**C**	☐ has
34. **A**	☐ able	**B**	☐ skilled	**C**	☐ possible
35. **A**	☐ last	**B**	☐ least	**C**	☐ all

Part 6

Questions 36–40
Read the descriptions of some documents/papers.
What is the word for each one?
The first letter is already there. There is one space for each other letter in the word.
For questions 36–40, write the words on your answer sheet.

Example:

0. The list of food in a restaurant: m e n u.

36. You sometimes need this document to travel abroad: p _ _ _ _ _ _ _.

37. The document which shows that you can drive a car: l _ _ _ _ _ _.

38. The paper which shows you have paid for transport on a train: t _ _ _ _ _.

39. A list that shows when trains or buses are running: t _ _ _ _ _ _ _ _.

40. To register or apply for something you must fill in a f _ _ _.

Part 7

Questions 41–50
Complete the email Oscar wrote to Tom.
Write ***one*** *word for each space.*
For questions 41–50, write the words on your answer sheet.

Example: (0) *to*

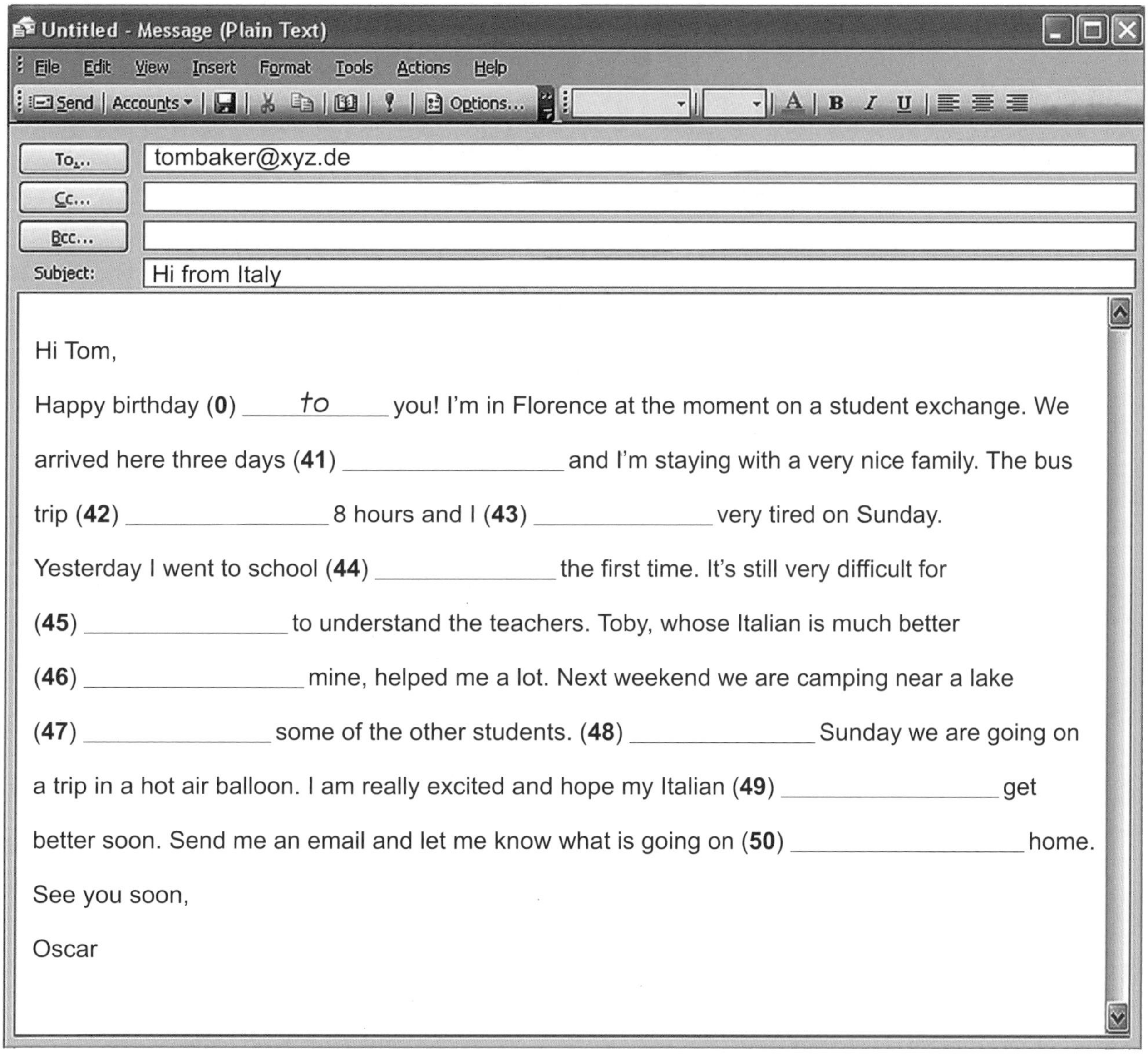

To: tombaker@xyz.de

Subject: Hi from Italy

Hi Tom,

Happy birthday (**0**) ___*to*___ you! I'm in Florence at the moment on a student exchange. We arrived here three days (**41**) ______________ and I'm staying with a very nice family. The bus trip (**42**) ______________ 8 hours and I (**43**) ______________ very tired on Sunday. Yesterday I went to school (**44**) ______________ the first time. It's still very difficult for (**45**) ______________ to understand the teachers. Toby, whose Italian is much better (**46**) ______________ mine, helped me a lot. Next weekend we are camping near a lake (**47**) ______________ some of the other students. (**48**) ______________ Sunday we are going on a trip in a hot air balloon. I am really excited and hope my Italian (**49**) ______________ get better soon. Send me an email and let me know what is going on (**50**) ______________ home.

See you soon,

Oscar

Part 8

Questions 51–55
Read the information and the note about the trip. It is organised by the local gardeners' club.
Fill in the information on the form.
For questions 51–55, write the information on your answer sheet.

04 April 2009

DEAR MEMBERS,

ON MAY 14 WE ARE TRAVELLING TO OXFORD. THIS YEAR WE HAVE PLANNED TWO DIFFERENT EVENTS. YOU CAN VISIT THE BOTANICAL GARDENS OR SEE A FLOWER SHOW. THE CLUB WILL PAY THE ENTRANCE FEES. IF YOU WANT TO TRAVEL BY BUS IT IS £15 FOR MEMBERS. YOU CAN BRING ONE OR TWO FRIENDS. BUT THEY'LL HAVE TO PAY £20 FOR THE BUS TRIP PER PERSON. PLEASE WRITE THEIR NAME(S) ON THE FORM. THERE IS ONE BUS FROM BIRMINGHAM (DEPARTURE 7 AM) AND ANOTHER ONE FROM COVENTRY (DEPARTURE 8 AM).

HENRIETTA PANSY

Gordon,

Could you please fill in the form?
I'd like to go by bus from Birmingham. I've always wanted to visit the botanical gardens. My friend Susan Polster is also coming. She is not a member of the gardeners' club.

Thanks and see you tomorrow,

Ruby

BOOKING FORM Gardeners' Club 2009 trip to Oxford

Name:		Ruby Hood
Date of trip:	**51**	
Departure from (city):	**52**	
Event:	**53**	
Name of 2nd person:	**54**	
Total cost for bus:	**55**	£ ________ for all people on this form

Part 9

Question 56

You are going to work in the garden this afternoon. Your friend Steve has promised to help. Send him an email.

Say:

- what you want to do in your garden
- when he should come
- what he should bring

Write 25–35 words.

Write the email on your answer sheet.

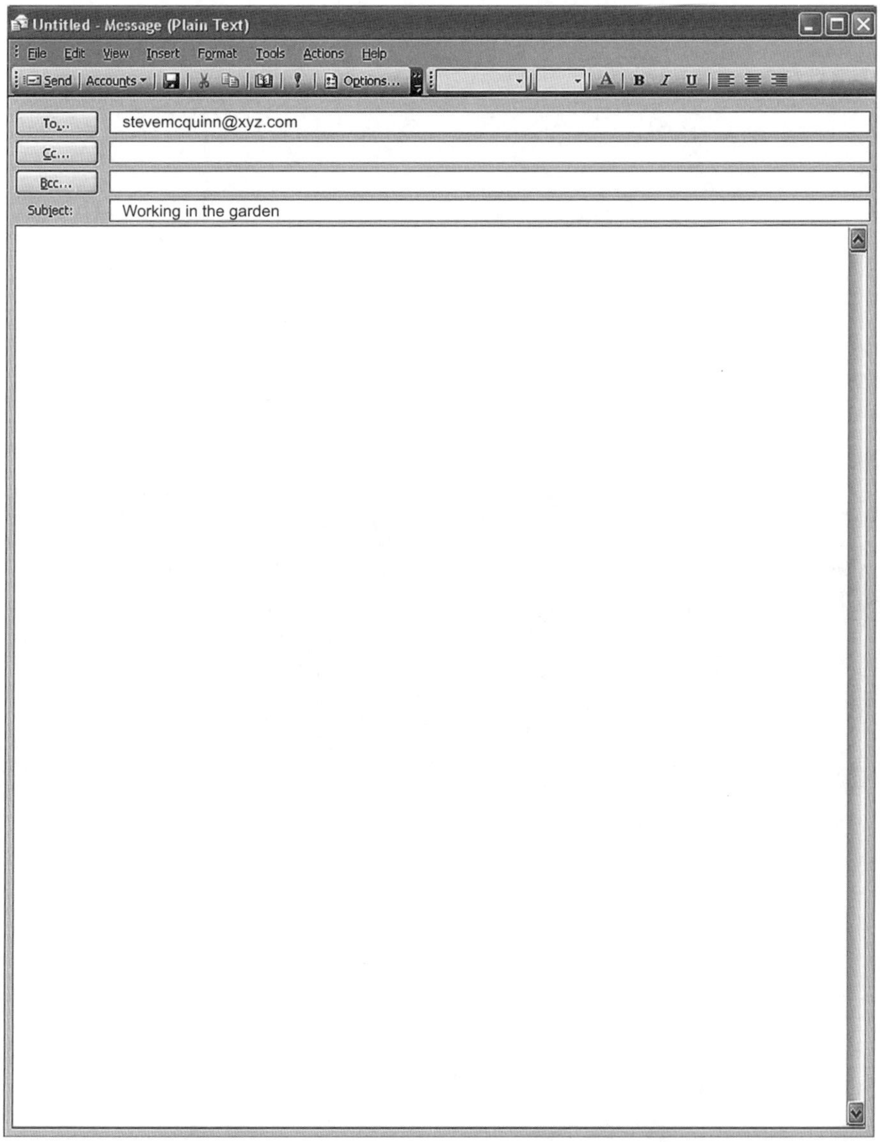

Paper 2: Listening

Part 1

Tracks 19–23

You will hear five short conversations.
You will hear each conversation twice.
There is one question for each conversation.
For questions 1–5, put a tick (✓) under the right answer.

Example:

0. When did the concert start?

WOMAN: Did the concert start at three o'clock yesterday?

MAN: No, they had planned to start at three thirty but the bus was late so they started at four.

A ☐

B ☐

C ☑

1. Where are they having a picnic?

A ☐

B ☐

C ☐

2. When is the school trip?

A ☐

B ☐

C ☐

3. Where do they sit in the restaurant?

A ☐

B ☐

C ☐

4. Which bag does Nick buy?

A ☐

B ☐

C ☐

5. How far is the zoo from the station?

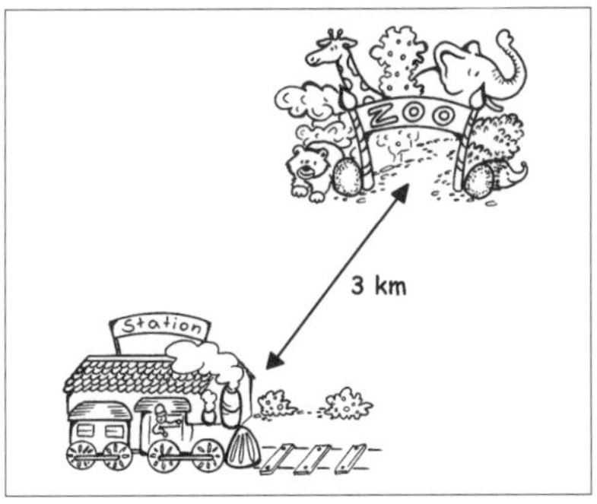

A ☐

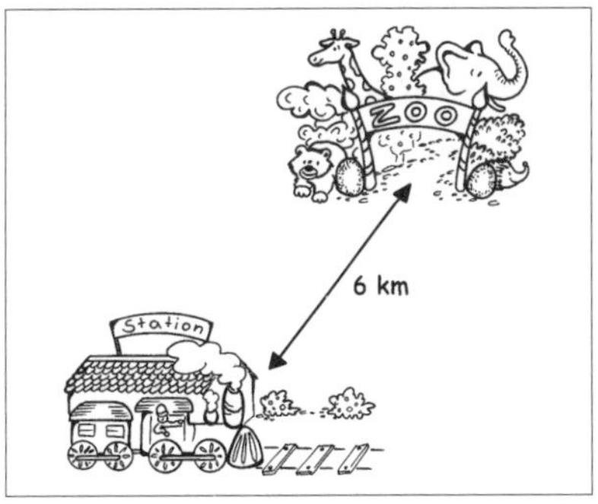

B ☐

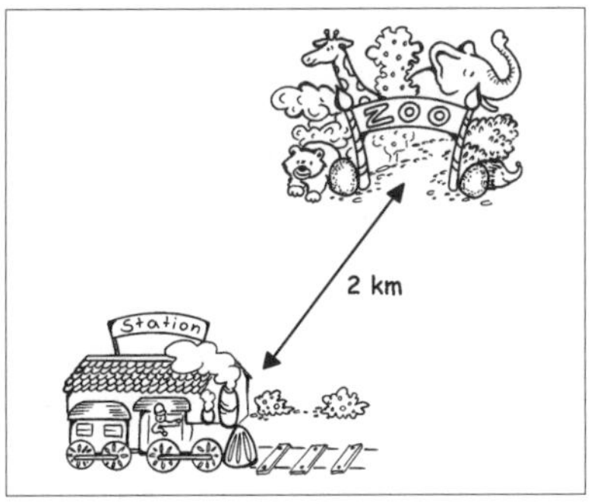

C ☐

Part 2

Track 24

Questions 6–10

Norman sometimes works at the local newsagent's after school. His friend Hannah is helping him today. They are making a list of the days on which the magazines come into the shop.

Listen and complete the list.

*For questions 6–10, write a letter (**A–H**) next to each day.*

You will hear the conversation twice.

Example:

0.	Saturday	A	**A**	TV magazines
6.	Monday	☐	**B**	Food & Cooking magazines
7.	Tuesday	☐	**C**	Children's magazines
8.	Wednesday	☐	**D**	Women's magazines
9.	Thursday	☐	**E**	Sports magazines
10.	Friday	☐	**F**	Music and Hobby magazines
			G	News magazines
			H	Magazines in foreign languages

Part 3

Track 25

Questions 11–15

Listen to Diana and Harold talking about a skiing trip at school.

*For questions 11–15, tick (✓) **A**, **B** or **C**.*

You will hear the conversation twice.

Example:

0. Diana was in the
   - **A** ☐ first group.
   - **B** ☐ second group.
   - **C** ☑ third group.

11. When did Diana's group travel?
    - **A** ☐ February
    - **B** ☐ March
    - **C** ☐ April

12. Where did they stay most nights?
    - **A** ☐ Guesthouse
    - **B** ☐ Youth hostel
    - **C** ☐ Hotel

13. What did the girls do in the town?
- **A** ☐ Go swimming
- **B** ☐ Write postcards
- **C** ☐ Go to a museum

14. What does Diana think about the swimming pool?
- **A** ☐ It's large and modern
- **B** ☐ It's expensive and modern
- **C** ☐ It's large and too cold

15. What did Diana enjoy most?
- **A** ☐ Swimming in the sun
- **B** ☐ Skiing in the sun
- **C** ☐ Sitting outside in the sun

Track 26

Part 4

Questions 16–20
You will hear a conversation about renting a bicycle.
Listen and complete questions 16–20.
You will hear the conversation twice.

BIKES & HIKES RENTAL SERVICE		
Rental period:		June 19–26
Sort of bike:	**16**	______________________
Size of person:	**17**	______________________ m
Bring bike to:	**18**	Beachside Hotel at __________ am
Price per day:	**19**	€ ______________
Name:	**20**	Brian ______________________

Track 27

Part 5

Questions 21–25
You will hear a recorded message.
Listen and complete questions 21–25.
You will hear the information twice.

Message from Photo Shop

Opening hours:	**21**	Monday – ______________ 9 am – 6 pm
New price per poster:	**22**	£ ______________
Postcards will arrive:	**23**	next ______________
Person to contact:	**24**	Chris ______________
Other material looks like:	**25**	______________

You now have 8 minutes to write your answers on the answer sheet.

Paper 3: Speaking

Part 1

Part 1 consists of a short conversation with the examiner. You should be familiar with the language associated with meeting people for the first time and you should be able to give information of a personal kind, e. g name, place of origin, occupation, family etc. You are also expected to talk about your daily life, your hobbies etc.

Part 2

Prompt cards are used to stimulate questions and answers. The examiner gives instructions and hands out a question card to one candidate and an answer card to the other. After the candidates have asked and answered their questions, they change roles.

Example

The examiner gives a question card to Candidate B and an answer card to Candidate A.

Candidate A, here is some information about factory outlet shopping.

Candidate B, you don't know anything about factory outlet shopping, so ask A some questions about it. Now B, ask A your questions about factory outlet shopping and A, you answer them.

Candidate A – your information.

FACTORY OUTLET
DESIGNER FASHION

28 Shops: clothes, shoes, bags & more

Free shuttle service to & from city centre every hour
Relaxing area with cafés and bistros

Call **info hotline 44 75 9 15** for fashion shows/events

Candidate B – your questions.

Factory Outlet Shopping

- How many shops?
- What/buy?
- How to get there?
- Food?
- More information?

Candidate B, here is some information about an indoor sports centre.

Candidate A, you don't know anything about this indoor sports centre, so ask B some questions about it. Now A, ask B your questions about it and B, you answer them.

Candidate B – your information.

Candidate A – your questions.

Indoor Sports Centre

- What/do?
- Opening hours?
- Cost?
- Specials?
- Do things outside?

Lösungsvorschläge

Reading and Writing

Part 1

1. To get a reduced price you must go here at a special time. **C**
2. Go here if you need your clothes cleaned quickly. **F**
3. You cannot go here every day. **H**
4. If you want to make a phone call, you have to go outside. **A**
5. You must pay cash for this service. **E**

Part 2

6. Each Saturday after … he meets his friends from the model railway club.
   A ☐ launch **B** ☐ lounge **C** ☑ lunch

7. His hobby is quite … but Mr Walters also builds a lot himself to save money.
   A ☐ cheap **B** ☐ valuable **C** ☑ expensive

8. His family give him a new locomotive as a Christmas … each year.
   A ☐ packet **B** ☑ present **C** ☐ package

9. Over the … he has built a huge model railway in the basement of his house.
   A ☑ years **B** ☐ times **C** ☐ ages

10. Next month Mr Walters wants to make a … to the railway museum with his friends.
    A ☐ travel **B** ☑ trip **C** ☐ voyage

Part 3

11. Can I go now?
    A ☐ After 2.30 pm.
    B ☐ No, I'll go there.
    C ☑ Yes, sure.

12. Where are you going this summer?
A ☐ Let's go then.
B ☑ We haven't decided yet.
C ☐ I prefer Spain.

13. How long are you going to stay in Brazil?
A ☑ For at least two weeks.
B ☐ The last two weeks.
C ☐ In two weeks.

14. Which pen is yours?
A ☐ This one is new.
B ☐ It doesn't matter.
C ☑ The blue one.

15. Say hello to Alison when you see her!
A ☐ Hello there.
B ☐ Yes, I like her.
C ☑ I will.

Robin: I'm fine, but I have to finish this report. I want to see the Polar Stars' ice-hockey match tonight.

Nina: 16. G

Robin: Yes, my sister gave it to me as a birthday present. I'm a big fan of the Polar Stars.

Nina: 17. H

Robin: Yes, and they have won the cup three times now. Why don't you come, too?

Nina 18. C

Robin: Oh yes, during the week they usually have some tickets left. The weekend matches are always sold out, though.

Nina: 19. E

Robin: At 5 pm. Why don't we meet at the ice-rink at 4 o'clock? We can get a ticket for you and meet my friends there.

Nina: 20. A

Robin: Well, see you later then.

Part 4

21. Lady Godiva did not want to help the poor people.
    A ☐ Right **B** ☑ Wrong **C** ☐ Doesn't say

22. The Earl did not think Lady Godiva would ride naked through the town.
    A ☑ Right **B** ☐ Wrong **C** ☐ Doesn't say

23. Some ladies helped Lady Godiva to comb her hair.
    A ☐ Right **B** ☐ Wrong **C** ☑ Doesn't say

24. Lady Godiva sent messengers round to tell the people what to do.
    A ☑ Right **B** ☐ Wrong **C** ☐ Doesn't say

25. Some people tried to watch her ride through Coventry.
    A ☐ Right **B** ☑ Wrong **C** ☐ Doesn't say

26. It took her four hours to ride through the town.
    A ☐ Right **B** ☐ Wrong **C** ☑ Doesn't say

27. After her ride the people of Coventry no longer had to pay taxes to Earl Leofric.
    A ☑ Right **B** ☐ Wrong **C** ☐ Doesn't say

Part 5

	A		B		C	
28.	☐	his	☐	them	☑	their
29.	☑	is	☐	was	☐	were
30.	☐	a	☑	both	☐	them
31.	☐	for	☑	to	☐	as
32.	☑	until	☐	by	☐	from
33.	☐	must	☐	have	☑	has
34.	☑	able	☐	skilled	☐	possible
35.	☐	last	☑	least	☐	all

Part 6

36. You sometimes need this document to travel abroad: **passport**.

37. The document which shows that you can drive a car: **license/licence**.

38. The paper which shows you have paid for transport on a train: **ticket**.

39. A list that shows when trains or buses are running: **timetable**.

40. To register or apply for something you must fill in a **form**.

Part 7

Hi Tom,
Happy birthday **to** you! I'm in Florence at the moment on a student exchange. We arrived here three days (**41**) **ago** and I'm staying with a very nice family. The bus trip (**42**) **took** 8 hours and I (**43**) **was** very tired on Sunday. Yesterday I went to school (**44**) **for** the first time. It's still very difficult for (**45**) **me (us)** to understand the teachers. Toby, whose Italian is much better (**46**) **than** mine, helped me a lot. Next weekend we are camping near a lake (**47**) **with** some of the other students. (**48**) **On** Sunday we are going on a trip in a hot air balloon. I am really excited and hope my Italian (**49**) **will** get better soon. Send me an email and let me know what is going on (**50**) **at** home.

See you soon,
Oscar

Part 8

Date of trip:	51	May 14
Departure from (city):	52	Birmingham
Event:	53	Botanical Gardens
Name of 2nd person:	54	Susan Polster
Total cost for bus:	55	£ 35 for all people on this form

Part 9

Hi Steve,

I would like to plant an apple tree and some bushes in my garden this afternoon. Can you come around 2 pm? Please bring another shovel and your radio..
Thanks and see you at 2!

Polly

Es müssen alle **drei Punkte** behandelt werden. Das Schreiben **muss mindestens 25 Worte** lang sein.

Listening

Tracks 19–23

Part 1

1. **Where are they having a picnic?**
   Woman: Shall we have our picnic over there near the water?
   Man: I think it might be nicer under the tree here. And it's probably not so hot.
   Woman: You're right, but there are old apples everywhere. Let's go and sit near those stones.
   Man: OK. Good idea.

2. **When is the school trip?**
   Girl: Have you heard that the date for the trip's been changed? It isn't May 26 anymore, it's June 16.
   Boy: Really? Why's that?
   Girl: Well, it turned out that class A 5 is going to be on a students' exchange until June 4.

3. **Where do they sit in the restaurant?**
   Man: I'd like to book a table for two for tonight for 8 o'clock. Could we have the table near the fireplace?
   Woman: I'm afraid that table's not available but I have a nice table on the terrace.
   Man: Hm. I think I'd prefer a table inside. Can we sit in the large room with the pictures?
   Woman: Yes, sure. Can I take your name?

4. **Which bag does Nick buy?**
   Girl: Hi Nick. What're you doing here?
   Boy: Oh, hi Pam. I need to get a new sports bag.
   Girl: Well, this one with the dots looks very nice.
   Boy: Yes, but I don't like it, it's for girls. I'll probably take the one with the stars and stripes.
   Girl: It's very large, though. Look, there's a rucksack.
   Boy: Now, this one's exactly what I was looking for. I'll take it.

5. **How far is the zoo from the station?**
BOY: Do you think we can walk to the zoo from the station?
GIRL: No, I think it's nearly 6 kilometres. My mum says it takes ages to walk there.
BOY: Really? Pete said there's a new path and it's only 2 kilometres now.
GIRL: Hold on. Here in the brochure it says "distance from station 3 kilometres". And there's a shuttle service, so we can decide when we get there.

1. Where are they having a picnic?

A ☑ B ☐ C ☐

2. When is the school trip?

A ☑ B ☐ C ☐

3. Where do they sit in the restaurant?

A ☐ B ☑ C ☐

4. Which bag does Nick buy?

A ☐ B ☐ C ☑

5. How far is the zoo from the station?

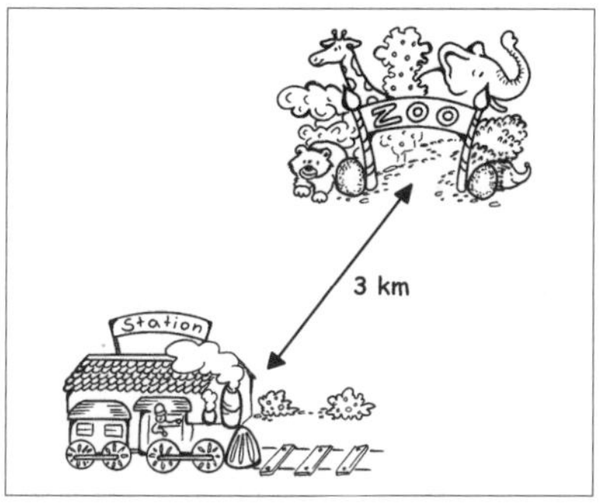

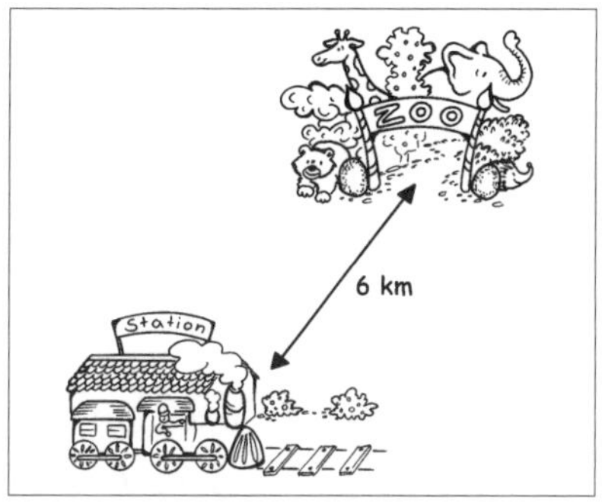

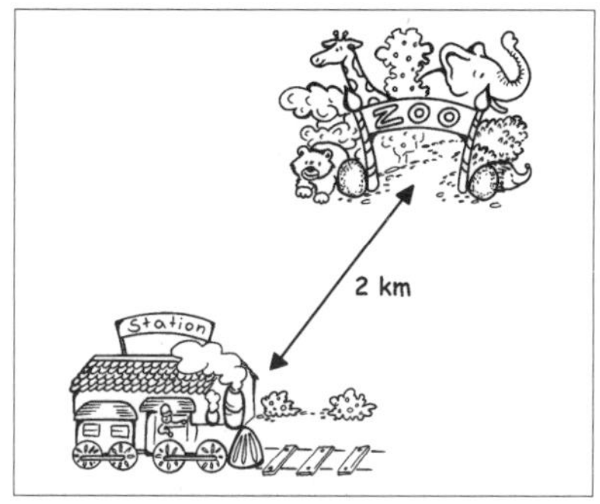

A ☑ B ☐ C ☐

Part 2

Tracks 24

NORMAN: Hi Hannah. Can you help me with this list?

HANNAH: Sure, but you know we´ve got to catch the bus at 5.

NORMAN: OK, then we'll be quick. I'll tell you the different sorts of magazines and the days they usually arrive.

HANNAH: Right. Fire away.

NORMAN: So these are the TV magazines. They always come on Saturday one week ahead.

HANNAH: Good. What's next?

NORMAN: Here we've got the news magazines. They arrive early on Monday morning. I think people like to read those on their way to work.

HANNAH: Hm. And what about the magazines for children?

NORMAN: They're delivered on Tuesday. No, wait Tuesday is the day for the women's magazines. There are lots of them and they arrive on Tuesday. That´s the largest pack of the week.

HANNAH: My mum's got a favourite magazine. Whenever she's reading it I'm not allowed to talk to her for at least an hour! So what about Thursday then?

NORMAN: Thursday's the day for the children's magazines. A lot of kids buy them on their way home from school. Ah, let's not forget the food and cooking magazines. There are more and more of those every week. They come in on Wednesday and some of them are really expensive.

HANNAH: Yes, but they do have nice photos. I always get hungry when I look at them!

NORMAN: I like the music magazines best. They're monthly magazines, though.

HANNAH: Yes, that's a pity. So, now I only have Friday left on my list.

NORMAN: Oh yes, of course, the sports magazines come on that day. My dad seems to take forever to read his football magazine!

6. Monday **G**
7. Tuesday **D**
8. Wednesday **B**
9. Thursday **C**
10. Friday **E**

Part 3

Tracks 25

HAROLD: Hi Diana. Already back from the skiing trip? Were you in the first or the second group?

DIANA: Actually, I was in the third group. We went in March but the snow was still fantastic.

HAROLD: Where did you stay?

DIANA: Well at first we stayed in a little guesthouse. But only for one night because there were problems with the heating. Then we moved to a nice hotel for the rest of the week.

HAROLD: Wow, that was lucky. Did you go skiing every day?

DIANA: Oh no. One day we went down to the town. Carla, Penny and I found a very nice café. We talked all afternoon and wrote postcards. Some others went to a museum.

HAROLD: Did you go to the new swimming pool, too?

DIANA: Yes, we did. It's really large and very modern.

HAROLD: And did you have good weather?

DIANA: Well, in the mornings it sometimes snowed a bit. It was sunny the whole week, though and I loved sitting outside in the sun after lunch. That was even better than skiing!

HAROLD: That sounds like you. Did you take many photos?

DIANA: Yes, I did. Susan took a lot too. We're all meeting at 3 in the school cafeteria to look at them. Join us if you like.

HAROLD: I'll be there!

11. When did Diana's group travel?
    - **A** [ ] February
    - **B** [✓] March
    - **C** [ ] April

12. Where did they stay most nights?
    - **A** [ ] Guesthouse
    - **B** [ ] Youth hostel
    - **C** [✓] Hotel

13. What did the girls do in the town?
- A ☐ Go swimming
- B ☑ Write postcards
- C ☐ Go to a museum

14. What does Diana think about the swimming pool?
- A ☑ It's large and modern
- B ☐ It's expensive and modern
- C ☐ It's large and too cold

15. What did Diana enjoy most?
- A ☐ Swimming in the sun
- B ☐ Skiing in the sun
- C ☑ Sitting outside in the sun

Part 4

Tracks 26

WOMAN: Good morning, Bikes & Hikes. How can I help you?

MAN: Good morning, I saw your site on the internet and I'd like to rent a bicycle for a week.

WOMAN: OK. When do you want the bike?

MAN: We arrive on June 12 and go hiking for one week. That means I'll need the bike from June 19 for 7 nights.

WOMAN: What sort of bike would you like? As you can see from our site we have a lot of different bikes, even tandems and electric bikes.

MAN: I think I'd prefer a mountain bike.

WOMAN: Yes, they're very good for getting round the island. The price is 15 Euros per day. Can you tell me how tall you are?

MAN: I'm about 1.80 m.

WOMAN: Alright, I think I've got the perfect bike for you. Will you pick it up here at our shop?

MAN: Well, would it be possible for you to bring the bike to the Beachside Hotel?

WOMAN: Sure, no problem we're just around the corner. When would you like it delivered?

MAN: Er … at around 8 am on June 19.

WOMAN: OK. I've made a note of that. Can I just take your name and credit card number?

MAN: Brian Hynkes. That's H Y N K E S. And the card number is 8394 9043 4940 3397.

Sort of bike:	16	mountain bike
Size of person:	17	1.80 m
Bring bike to:	18	Beachside Hotel at 8 am
Price per day:	19	€ 15
Name:	20	Brian Hynkes

Part 5

Tracks 27

Good morning. This is the Photo Shop on High Street. You ordered some posters and postcards from us. The posters arrived this morning. You can come and pick them up at any time. We're open from Monday to Saturday from 9 am to 6 pm. As you ordered 10 posters we can give you a special price. That's £5 per poster and not £5.90 as I told you before.
Unfortunately the postcards you wanted haven't arrived yet. The printer has promised to bring them next week. I think you told me that you wanted these 25 postcards as invitations for a wedding.
If next week is too late, please call us. Just ask for Chris Scott. We could have the postcards printed on different material, which looks like leather and the price is the same. Thank you.

Opening hours:	**21**	Monday – *Saturday* 9 am – 6 pm
New price per poster:	**22**	£ *5.00*/£ *5*
Postcards will arrive:	**23**	next *week*
Person to contact:	**24**	Chris *Scott*
Other material looks like:	**25**	*leather*

Speaking

Part 2

THERESA (CANDIDATE B): Can you tell me more about the **factory outlet**?
JOHANNES (CANDIDATE A): Yes, of course, what would you like to know?
THERESA (CANDIDATE B): How many shops are there?
JOHANNES (CANDIDATE A): There are 28 shops in total.
THERESA (CANDIDATE B): And what can you buy there?
JOHANNES (CANDIDATE A): You can buy clothes, shoes, bags and so on.
THERESA (CANDIDATE B): How do I get to the factory outlet?
JOHANNES (CANDIDATE A): There's a free shuttle service from the city centre.
THERESA (CANDIDATE B): Can you get something to eat there? (Do they also sell food?/Are there any restaurants?)
JOHANNES (CANDIDATE A): Yes, there are cafés and bistros.
THERESA (CANDIDATE B): Where can I get more information? (Do you have more information?)
JOHANNES (CANDIDATE A): There's an info hotline for shows and events. (You can call the info hotline to find out about shows and events.)
THERESA (CANDIDATE B): Thank you very much.
JOHANNES (CANDIDATE A): You're welcome.

JOHANNES (CANDIDATE A): Do you have information on the **indoor sports centre**?
THERESA (CANDIDATE B): Yes, of course. What would you like to know about it?
JOHANNES (CANDIDATE A): Well, first I'd like to know what you can do there? (What can you do there?)
THERESA (CANDIDATE B): You can use all attractions (and gear is included).
JOHANNES (CANDIDATE A): Do you know when it is open? (What are the opening hours?/Do you have information on the opening hours?)
THERESA (CANDIDATE B): It's open daily from 10 am to 7 pm/from 10 in the morning to 7 in the evening.
JOHANNES (CANDIDATE A): (That's good.) And how much is it? (And do you know the prices they charge?)
THERESA (CANDIDATE B): It's 7 pounds for adults and 5.50 for teenagers under 18.
JOHANNES (CANDIDATE A): Are there any specials?
THERESA (CANDIDATE B): Yes, you get free admission and a cake on your birthday. (You don't have to pay anything on your birthday [and you even get a cake.])
JOHANNES (CANDIDATE A): Can you also do things outside?
THERESA (CANDIDATE B): Yes, there is a climbing garden which is open from May to September.
JOHANNES (CANDIDATE A): Thanks a lot for all the information.
THERESA (CANDIDATE B): That's OK.

Sprachenzertifikat Englisch A2
Mock Exam 4

Paper 1: Reading and Writing

Part 1

Questions 1–5
*Which notice (**A–H**) says this (**1–5**)?*
*For questions 1–5, mark the correct letters **A–H** on your answer sheet.*

Example:

0. These things are not good for small children. **B**

1. If you want to eat something outside, you must not be too late. ☐
2. There is a special area for your bags, jackets etc. ☐
3. The timetable changes from season to season. ☐
4. You must be quick if you want to take part in this event. ☐
5. You are not allowed to let in fresh air for security reasons. ☐

A ➡ **Fresh bread**
at half-price after 5 pm

B Toys not good for children under 3 years

C **Ferry times**
summer every hour (9 am – 4 pm)
winter: 3 × daily (9 am / 11 am / 2 pm)

D **alarm system in operation**
keep windows closed at all times

E **school trip to London**
– only few seats left –

F bikes & fun vehicles for rent

G *drinks always available from bar*
We do not serve food outdoors after 5 pm

H please leave your belongings here

Part 2

Questions 6–10
Read the sentences about sandboarding.
*Choose the best word (**A, B** or **C**) for each space.*
*For questions 6–10, mark **A, B** or **C** on your answer sheet.*

Example:

0. Carol thinks sandboarding is the most … sport in the world.
   A ☐ favourite **B** ☐ fun **C** ☑ exciting

6. She loves … down the hill in her helmet and summer clothes.
   A ☐ climbing **B** ☐ racing **C** ☐ rocking

7. It is a good sport for young people because you can rent all the …
   A ☐ goods **B** ☐ board **C** ☐ equipment

8. Carol has already won the first … in a competition twice.
   A ☐ place **B** ☐ prize **C** ☐ cup

9. A reporter from a famous sports magazine … some photos and wrote a story about Carol.
   A ☐ made **B** ☐ took **C** ☐ clicked

10. When she finishes school, Carol … to become a test person for sandboards and snowboards.
    A ☐ wants **B** ☐ will **C** ☐ loves

Part 3

Questions 11–15
Complete the five conversations.
*For questions 11–15, mark **A, B** or **C** on your answer sheet.*

Example:

0. Did you understand what the teacher said?
   A ☐ Nothing special.
   B ☑ Not really.
   C ☐ It's not enough.

11. I'm hungry. Let's have a sandwich.
    A ☐ Yes, very much so.
    B ☐ Good idea!
    C ☐ Don't mention it.

12. Have you spoken to Jim?
- **A** ☐ I saw her yesterday.
- **B** ☐ It's a pity.
- **C** ☐ Not yet.

13. Is Elena coming to your party?
- **A** ☐ She loves dancing.
- **B** ☐ I don't think so.
- **C** ☐ No, not at all.

14. I'm going to the supermarket.
- **A** ☐ Don't mention it.
- **B** ☐ Forget it!
- **C** ☐ Don't forget the lemons.

15. Have a nice weekend!
- **A** ☐ And you too.
- **B** ☐ Yes, I like it.
- **C** ☐ You're welcome.

Questions 16–20
Complete the conversation.
What does Astrid say to Uma?
*For questions 16–20, mark the correct letter **A–H** on your answer sheet.*

Example:

Astrid: Hello Uma. How are you?

Uma: **0.** C

Astrid: Oh, what a pity. Shall I help you find them?

Uma: **16.** ______

Astrid: Hm, what were you doing?

Uma: **17.** ______

Astrid: And you were here all the time?

Uma: **18.** ______

Astrid: Why don't you go and ask at the shop and I'll go on searching here?

Uma: **19.** ______

Astrid: You do look happy! Have you found your keys?

Uma: **20.** ______

Astrid: Well, you were really lucky! What about another ice-cream?

A That would be great. They must be somewhere round here.

B Yes, I must have left them on the counter when I took out the money for the ice-cream. The old lady in the shop was very nice.

C Not too good. I've lost my keys.

D No, I wasn't. I bought some ice-cream over there.

E Can you help me?

F And how did it happen?

G We were playing frisbee and then everyone went home for lunch.

H Good idea, I'll be back in a minute.

Part 4

Questions 21–27
Read Peter's story and then answer the questions.
*For questions 21–27, mark **A**, **B** or **C** on your answer sheet.*

My name is Peter Jefferson. I come from a small town in Sweden but I have been living in England for many years. When I came to England I was a student. I wanted to become an architect but I never really enjoyed studying. Then, a friend from university asked me if I could help him sell food in my free time. His dad had a small hamburger shop. I really liked the job and enjoyed talking to the people. Soon I bought an old van and spent about a month to make some changes and clean it. When it was ready it really looked good and I was a successful businessman from the beginning. People liked my hot dogs. Everyone got exactly the hot dog they wanted. Soon I bought another van because the price was very good. Today I have five vans in three towns and seven people working for me. I still love my job. In the first years I worked really hard. Now I go on holiday two or three times a year. I love water-skiing and spent a week in Greece last year to learn diving. When I retire I'd like to learn the Greek language and live there.

Example:

0. Peter comes from
   A ☐ Denmark.
   B ☑ Sweden.
   C ☐ England.

21. When he came to England he was a(n)
   A ☐ architect.
   B ☐ teacher.
   C ☐ student.

22. Peter
   A ☐ liked studying a lot.
   B ☐ did not like studying.
   C ☐ studied from home.

23. A friend asked him
   A ☐ to sell hot dogs.
   B ☐ to help him with his studies.
   C ☐ to sell hamburgers.

24. Peter soon decided
- **A** ☐ to work with people.
- **B** ☐ to open his own business.
- **C** ☐ to repair vans.

25. People liked Peter's hot dogs because
- **A** ☐ everyone got what they wanted.
- **B** ☐ Peter was a successful businessman.
- **C** ☐ the price was good.

26. Today Peter has
- **A** ☐ seven employees.
- **B** ☐ seven vans.
- **C** ☐ five employees and seven vans.

27. Last year Peter took
- **A** ☐ water-skiing lessons.
- **B** ☐ Greek lessons.
- **C** ☐ diving lessons.

Part 5

Questions 28–35

*Read the text about Ocarinas. Choose the best word (**A**, **B** or **C**) for each space.*

*For questions 28–35, mark **A**, **B** or **C** on your answer sheet.*

OCARINAS

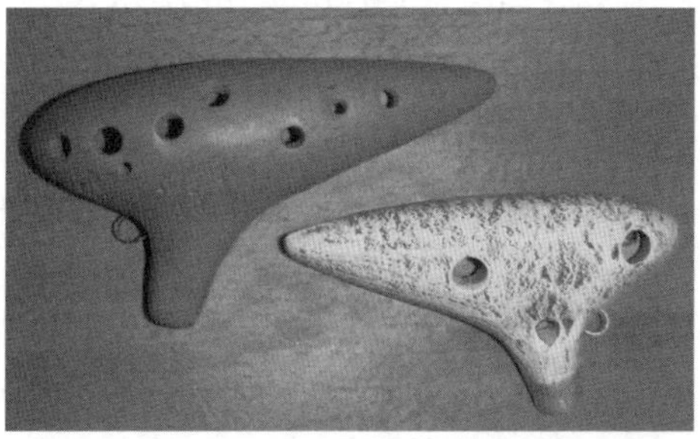

Ocarinas (0) ___are___ musical instruments made of clay or sometimes of wood. They are small flutes and (28) ____________ look like animals or birds. In Italian the (29) ____________ Ocarina means "little goose". The Ocarinas we (30) ____________ today were first built in Italy about 150 years ago. Early versions (31) ____________ the instrument were already played thousands of years ago. They were often very simple flutes in the shape of (32) ____________ egg. An Ocarina has four (33) ____________ twelve holes and is played with both hands. In Italy and Austria there are many people who still play the instrument (34) ____________ day. Can you believe that there (35) ____________ even a computer game in which an Ocarina plays an important role?

Example:

	A		B		C	
0.	☐	some	☑	are	☐	one
28.	☐	much	☐	often	☐	than
29.	☐	word	☐	instrument	☐	note
30.	☐	knows	☐	knowing	☐	know
31.	☐	of	☐	some	☐	from
32.	☐	some	☐	an	☐	a
33.	☐	by	☐	to	☐	and
34.	☐	no	☐	some	☐	every
35.	☐	are	☐	were	☐	is

Part 6

Questions 36–40
Read the descriptions of some things you can see at an airport.
What is the word for each one?
The first letter is already there. There is one space for each other letter in the word.
For questions 36–40, write the words on your answer sheet.

Example:

0. You need this piece of paper to get on the plane. t i c k e t

36. Many travellers carry their clothes in a s _ _ _ _ _ _ _ _.

37. People who travel for fun are also called t _ _ _ _ _ _ _ _.

38. Many businesspeople pay their tickets by c _ _ _ _ _ _ _ _ _ _.

39. When a plane arrives late this is called a d _ _ _ _.

40. The small bags you can take on the plane are called hand l _ _ _ _ _ _.

Part 7

Questions 41–50
Complete the email Archie wrote about a trip he will make with his friend next week.
*Write **one** word for each space.*
For questions 41–50, write the words on your answer sheet.

Example: (0) *have*

Untitled - Message (Plain Text)

File Edit View Insert Format Tools Actions Help

To... toby@web.com

Cc...

Bcc...

Subject: Our trip next week

Hi Toby,

I (**0**) *have* just received the programme for our trip next week. On Sunday we (**41**) ________ arrive at about 7 pm. There is going to (**42**) ________ a barbecue for everyone. On Monday we will walk up to the castle, which will take about three (**43**) ________. On Tuesday we (**44**) ________ do what we want. I (**45**) ________ like to go to the pool if the weather is good enough. (**46**) ________ do you think? I (**47**) ________ really looking forward to Wednesday, (**48**) ________ we are going to the theme park on that day. My sister visited it (**49**) ________ week and she loved it! She said it was the (**50**) ________ place she has ever been to.

See you soon,

Archie

Part 8

Questions 51–55
Read the advert and the letter.
Fill in the correct information for Maureen on the Candidate Information Sheet.
For questions 51–55, write the information on your answer sheet.

Would you like to help at the local summer camp for children?

We need students for July and August.
Possible hours from 6 am to 8 pm.
Must be at least 18 years old.

Write to Ms Warner giving the number of hours you can work per week.

Dear Ms Warner,

My name is Maureen Henderson.

I am 19 years old and my school holidays start on July 12. I would like to work for three weeks, 24-30 hours a week. I like getting up early, so I would not mind preparing breakfast.

Yours sincerely,

Maureen

M.Henderson@xyz.co.uk

Candidate Information Sheet – Holiday job at the summer camp

Name:		Maureen Henderson, 19 years old
Contact or address:	**51**	
Possible start date:	**52**	
Hours per week:	**53**	
Number of weeks:	**54**	
Preferred job(s):	**55**	

Part 9

Question 56
You want to buy a new computer on Friday. Your friend Antonia knows a lot about computers. Write her an email.

Tell her:
- what you want to do on Friday
- what you need the computer for
- where you want to meet her

Write 25–35 words.
Write the email on your answer sheet.

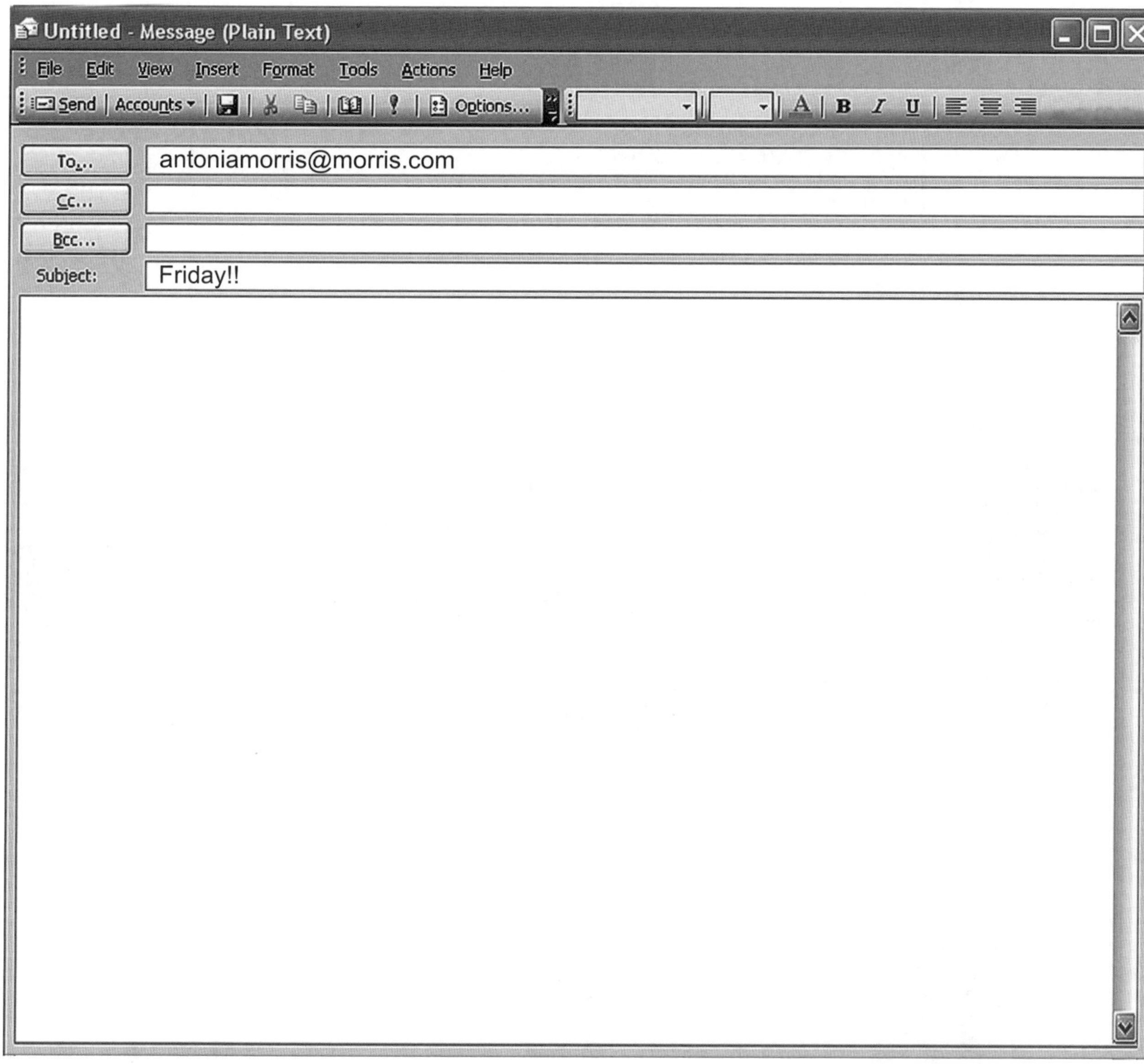

Paper 2: Listening

Part 1

Tracks 28–32

You will hear five short conversations.
You will hear each conversation twice.
There is one question for each conversation.
For questions 1–5, put a tick (✓) under the right answer.

Example:

0. When did the concert start?

WOMAN: Did the concert start at three o'clock yesterday?

MAN: No, they had planned to start at three thirty but the bus was late so they started at four.

A ☐

B ☐

C ☑

1. Where is the bird now?

A ☐

B ☐

C ☐

2. When will they look at the new car?

A ☐

B ☐

C ☐

3. What is Paul collecting?

A ☐

B ☐

C ☐

4. Which sofa is Susan going to buy?

A ☐

B ☐

C ☐

5. What did the girl enjoy most on the school trip?

A ☐

B ☐

C ☐

Part 2

Track 33

Questions 6–10

The Hoods are going to paint the rooms of their new house. They are talking about the different colours they are going to use for each room.
Listen and complete the list.
*For questions 6–10, write a letter (**A–H**) next to each part of the house.*
You will hear the conversation twice.

Example:

0. sitting room	G	**A**	pink
6. kitchen	☐	**B**	grey
7. balcony	☐	**C**	blue
8. Paul's room	☐	**D**	yellow
9. bathroom	☐	**E**	green
10. bedroom	☐	**F**	orange
		G	white
		H	red

Part 3

Track 34

Questions 11–15
Listen to Romy and Ken talking about a day at the zoo.
*For questions 11–15, tick (✓) **A**, **B** or **C**.*
You will hear the conversation twice.

Example:

0. Ken is going to the zoo this
   - **A** ☐ Thursday.
   - **B** ☑ Tuesday.
   - **C** ☐ Monday.

11. How did Romy get to the zoo?
   - **A** ☐ bus
   - **B** ☐ train
   - **C** ☐ taxi

12. When they arrived it was
   - **A** ☐ sunny.
   - **B** ☐ raining.
   - **C** ☐ windy.

What did Romy like most?

A ☐ starfish
B ☐ shells
C ☐ colourful fish

14. What did Romy buy at the zoo shop?

A ☐ T-shirt and a soft drink
B ☐ T-shirt and ice-cream
C ☐ Postcards

15. Romy thought the postcards were

A ☐ not nice at all.
B ☐ too expensive.
C ☐ not expensive.

Part 4

Track 35

Questions 16–20
You will hear a conversation about a birthday cake.
Listen and complete questions 16–20.
You will hear the conversation twice.

Cake Paradise		
Date cake(s) will be collected:		May 7
Football cake for 8 people, Players on cake made of	**16**	____________
Do **not** put	**17**	____________ in the cake
Other cakes:	**18**	____________ cream cake
Total cost incl. box:	**19**	£ ____________
Name of customer:	**20**	____________

Part 5

Track 36

Questions 21–25
You will hear a recorded phone message.
Listen and complete questions 21–25.
You will hear the information twice.

Peter's DIY		
New colour:	21	______
New price:	22	£ ______
Shop assistant's name:	23	______
Sizes of overalls:	24	M and ______
Special offer:	25	______ % off all brushes and rollers

You now have 8 minutes to write your answers on the answer sheet.

Paper 3: Speaking

Part 1

Part 1 consists of a short conversation with the examiner. You should be familiar with the language associated with meeting people for the first time and you should be able to give information of a personal kind, e. g name, place of origin, occupation, family etc. You are also expected to talk about your daily life, your hobbies etc.

Part 2

Prompt cards are used to stimulate questions and answers. The examiner gives instructions and hands out a questions card to one candidate and an answer card to the other. After the candidates have asked and answered their questions, they change roles.

Example

The examiner gives a question card to Candidate B and an answer card to Candidate A.

Candidate A, here is some information about painting lessons.

Candidate B, you don't know anything about painting lessons, so ask A some questions about it. Now B, ask A your questions about painting lessons and A, you answer them.

Candidate A – your information.

*Classes for **teenagers** every afternoon 2 – 4 pm*
*Bring **brushes** and **paper** · wear **old clothes***
*Only **£ 75** for ten lessons*
*Call **93 72 47** and start tomorrow*

Candidate B – your questions.

Painting Lessons

- Where?
- When?
- Bring anything?
- Cost?
- Telephone?

Candidate B, here is some information about Mega Diggers.

Candidate A, you don't know anything about Mega Diggers, so ask B some questions about it. Now A, ask B your questions about Mega Diggers and B, you answer them.

Candidate B – your information.

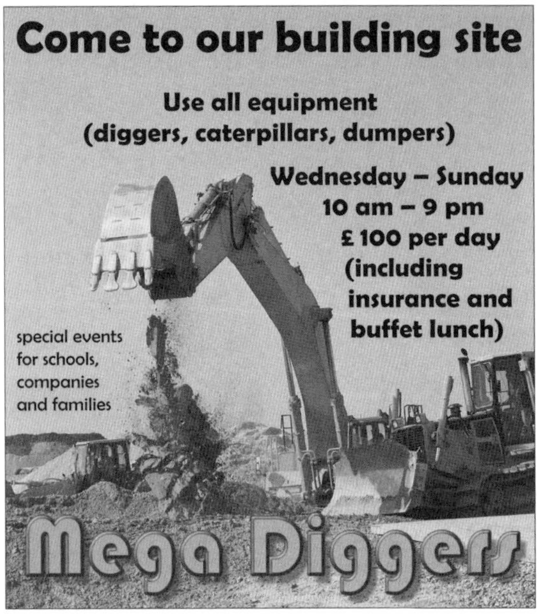

Candidate A – your questions.

Mega Diggers

- What to do there?
- Cost?
- What/included?
- Opening hours?
- Special arrangements?

Lösungsvorschläge

Reading and Writing

Part 1

1. If you want to eat something outside, you must not be too late. **G**
2. There is a special area for your bags, jackets etc. **H**
3. The timetable changes from season to season. **C**
4. You must be quick if you want to take part in this event. **E**
5. You are not allowed to let in fresh air for security reasons. **D**

Part 2

6. She loves … down the hill in her helmet and summer clothes.
   A ☐ climbing **B** ☑ racing **C** ☐ rocking

7. It is a good sport for young people because you can rent all the …
   A ☐ goods **B** ☐ board **C** ☑ equipment

8. Carol has already won the first … in a competition twice.
   A ☐ place **B** ☑ prize **C** ☐ cup

9. A reporter from a famous sports magazine … some photos and wrote a story about Carol.
   A ☐ made **B** ☑ took **C** ☐ clicked

10. When she finishes school, Carol … to become a test person for sandboards and snowboards.
    A ☑ wants **B** ☐ will **C** ☐ loves

Part 3

11. I'm hungry. Let's have a sandwich.
    A ☐ Yes, very much so.
    B ☑ Good idea!
    C ☐ Don't mention it.

12. Have you spoken to Jim?
    A ☐ I saw her yesterday.
    B ☐ It's a pity.
    C ☑ Not yet.

13. Is Elena coming to your party?
- A ☐ She loves dancing.
- B ☑ I don't think so.
- C ☐ No, not at all.

14. I'm going to the supermarket.
- A ☐ Don't mention it.
- B ☐ Forget it!
- C ☑ Don't forget the lemons.

15. Have a nice weekend!
- A ☑ And you too.
- B ☐ Yes, I like it.
- C ☐ You're welcome.

Astrid: Oh, what a pity. Shall I help you find them?

Uma: **16.** A

Astrid: Hm, what were you doing?

Uma: **17.** G

Astrid: And you were here all the time?

Uma: **18.** D

Astrid: Why don't you go and ask at the shop and I'll go on searching here?

Uma: **19.** H

Astrid: You do look happy! Have you found your keys?

Uma: **20.** B

Astrid: Well, you were really lucky! What about another ice-cream?

Part 4

21. When he came to England he was a(n)
- A ☐ architect.
- B ☐ teacher.
- C ☑ student.

22. Peter
- A ☐ liked studying a lot.
- B ☑ did not like studying.
- C ☐ studied from home.

23. A friend asked him
- A ☐ to sell hot dogs.
- B ☐ to help him with his studies.
- C ☑ to sell hamburgers.

24. Peter soon decided
- A ☐ to work with people.
- B ☑ to open his own business.
- C ☐ to repair vans.

25. People liked Peter's hot dogs because
- A ☑ everyone got what they wanted.
- B ☐ Peter was a successful businessman.
- C ☐ the price was good.

26. Today Peter has
- A ☑ seven employees.
- B ☐ seven vans.
- C ☐ five employees and seven vans.

27. Last year Peter took
- A ☐ water skiing lessons.
- B ☐ Greek lessons.
- C ☑ diving lessons.

Part 5

	A	B	C
28.	☐ much	☑ often	☐ than
29.	☑ word	☐ instrument	☐ note
30.	☐ knows	☐ knowing	☑ know
31.	☑ of	☐ some	☐ from
32.	☐ some	☑ an	☐ a
33.	☐ by	☑ to	☐ and
34.	☐ no	☐ some	☑ every
35.	☐ are	☐ were	☑ is

Part 6

36. Many travellers carry their clothes in a **suitcase**.

37. The people who travel for fun are also called **tourists**.

38. Many businesspeople pay their tickets by **credit card**.

39. When a plane arrives late this is called a **delay**.

40. The small bags you can take on the plane are called hand **luggage**.

Part 7

Hi Toby,
I **have** just received the programme for our trip next week. On Sunday we (**41**) **will** arrive at about 7 pm. There is going to (**42**) **be** a barbecue for everyone. On Monday we will walk up to the castle, which will take about three (**43**) **hours**. On Tuesday we (**44**) **can** do what we want. I (**45**) **would/'d** like to go to the pool if the weather is good enough. (**46**) **What** do you think? I (**47**) **am/'m** really looking forward to Wednesday, (**48**) **because/as** we are going to the theme park on that day. My sister visited it (**49**) **last** week and she loved it! She said it was the (**50**) **best** place she has ever been to.

See you soon,
Archie

Part 8

Contract or address:	**51**	M.Henderson@xyz.co.uk
Possible start date:	**52**	July 12
Hours per week:	**53**	24 - 30
Number of weeks:	**54**	three/3
Preferred job(s):	**55**	making/preparing breakfast

Part 9

Dear Antonia,

I need to buy a new computer to write my reports. Would you like to come and help me? Can we meet at the shopping centre at 3 pm on Friday?
Love,

Monika

Es müssen alle **drei Punkte** behandelt werden. Das Schreiben **muss mindestens 25 Worte** lang sein.

Listening

Part 1

Tracks 28–32

1. **Where is the bird now?**
   Woman: Look, can you see the little bird?
   Man: The brown one near the pool?
   Woman: No, the little yellow one. It was sitting on the grass and now it's gone!
   Man: Look, it's sitting on the tree now.
   Woman: Ah yes, now I see it.

2. **When will they look at the new car?**
   Man: Are you free on Tuesday to look at the new car?
   Woman: No, I'm sorry. Can we go on Wednesday?
   Man: No, I'm working until 7. How about Thursday?
   Woman: That's fine with me. Let's meet at the station at 2.

3. **What is Paul collecting?**
   Woman: Are you still collecting stamps, Paul?
   Man: No, I never did. I used to collect coins for a while.
   Woman: And now?
   Man: Well, now I'm collecting old postcards. They're much more interesting than the coins.

4. **Which sofa is Susan going to buy?**
   Man: What do you think of the grey sofa?
   Woman: I don't like grey. I like the one with the flowers, but it's too big for my room.
   Man: Why don't you take this one here with the stripes then?
   Woman: Good idea, and the colour's very nice, too.

5. **What did the girl enjoy most on the school trip?**

BOY: And did you also visit the castle?

GIRL: Yes, on Monday and it was really interesting. But what I liked most was the zoo. I just love animals.

BOY: Did you look at all the old ships in the museum?

GIRL: Yes, the boys really liked it.

1. Where is the bird now?

A ☑ B ☐ C ☐

2. When will they look at the new car?

A ☑ B ☐ C ☐

3. What is Paul collecting?

A ☐ B ☑ C ☐

4. Which sofa is Susan going to buy?

A ☐

B ☐

C ☑

5. What did the girl enjoy most on the school trip?

A ☑

B ☐

C ☐

Part 2

Tracks 33

MR HOOD: Right, let's decide about the colours for the rooms. What about yellow for the sitting room?
MRS HOOD: I think the sitting room should be white.
MR HOOD: OK, you're right with all the furniture and pictures. And the kitchen? Maybe pink?
MRS HOOD: No, I hate pink. I wanted the kitchen yellow or green.
MR HOOD: Yellow sounds nice. Green's better for the balcony. What do you think?
MRS HOOD: Yes, a fresh green would be nice with all my plants.
MR HOOD: OK, and Paul's room?
MRS HOOD: I think he likes grey best.
MR HOOD: Perhaps blue would be better for all his ships and pirates.
MRS HOOD: Hm, that's true. So let's make it blue then.
MR HOOD: First I wanted blue for the bathroom but now I'd prefer orange.
MRS HOOD: That's fine with me, orange will wake you up in the morning!
MR HOOD: OK, what else do we need?
MRS HOOD: A relaxing colour for the bedroom. How about yellow?
MR HOOD: No, I wouldn't like that. I think a light grey would be much better.
MRS HOOD: I agree with you.

6. kitchen **D**
7. balcony **E**
8. Paul's room **C**
9. bathroom **F**
10. bedroom **B**

Part 3

Tracks 34

ROMY: Hi Ken. Did your class visit the zoo last Monday, too?
KEN: No, we're going this Tuesday.
ROMY: Oh yes, I forgot you had exams until last Thursday.
KEN: Tell me about it. Anyway, did you go by train?
ROMY: No, we went by bus but it broke down, so Mrs Brannick just got taxis for us.
KEN: That's funny! Which animals did you see?
ROMY: When we arrived it was raining so we went to the sea water aquarium first.
KEN: Was it interesting?
ROMY: Oh yes, all the fish and shells – it was so colourful! I liked the starfish best, they're just fantastic.
KEN: I hope we'll have time to look at the aquarium. Everyone says it's great! What did you do next?
ROMY: Well, by then it had stopped raining and we walked around and saw all sorts of animals. Then we had a break and I bought some ice-cream and a T-shirt from the zoo shop.
KEN: Didn't you buy postcards of the little polar bear?
ROMY: I wanted to take my own photos, but first it was in the cave and when it came out, there were too many people. So in the end I bought some postcards from a guide.
KEN: Good idea.
ROMY: Yes, the postcards are really nice and weren't expensive at all.

11. How did Romy get to the zoo?
    A ☐ bus
    B ☐ train
    C ☑ taxi

12. When they arrived it was
    A ☐ sunny.
    B ☑ raining.
    C ☐ windy.

13. What did Romy like most?
    A ☑ starfish
    B ☐ shells
    C ☐ colourful fish

14. What did Romy buy at the zoo shop?
- A ☐ T-shirt and a soft drink
- B ☑ T-shirt and ice-cream
- C ☐ postcards

15. Romy thought the postcards were
- A ☐ not nice at all.
- B ☐ too expensive.
- C ☑ not expensive.

Part 4

Tracks 35

MAN: Good morning, Cake Paradise. How can I help you?
WOMAN: I'd like to order a cake for my son's birthday.
MAN: Right, when do you want the cake?
WOMAN: Well, the birthday party is on the 8th but I think I'd like to collect it on the evening of the 7th.
MAN: OK, no problem, we're open until 7 pm. What sort of cake would you like?
WOMAN: Can you give me a few ideas?
MAN: Sure, er … what are your son's hobbies?
WOMAN: Swimming and football.
MAN: Then I think a football cake with little players made of sugar would be very nice.
WOMAN: Yes, that sounds very good. We need the cake for 6, no, 8 people.
MAN: OK, no problem.
WOMAN: Oh, and can you make sure there are no strawberries in the cake? My husband doesn't like them.
MAN: Right, I'll make a note. Do you need anything else?
WOMAN: Oh yes, I'd also like a small chocolate cream cake for four people.
MAN: Alright, we'll have everything ready for you on the 7th in the afternoon. Can I take your name, please?
WOMAN: Yes, it's Peekes. That's P- double E – K – E – S. How much will it cost?
MAN: It'll be £ 13 in total. If you'd like a nice box for the big cake, that's £ 2 extra.
WOMAN: Alright, I'll take a box, because it's a present.

Football cake for 8 people, Players on cake made of	16	*sugar*
Do **not** put	17	*strawberries* in the cake
Other cakes:	18	*chocolate* cream cake
Total cost incl. box:	19	*£15*
Name of customer:	20	*PEEKES*

Part 5

Tracks 36

Good afternoon, this is Peter's DIY. I just wanted to tell you that the paint you ordered arrived yesterday. I'm very sorry, but they didn't send exactly the quality we ordered. It's no longer produced, I'm afraid. The paint I have here looks more like cream rather than pearly white. Perhaps you can have a look at it, then decide what you want to do. The price is only £ 12 instead of £ 16 for the white paint.
I won't be in the shop this Saturday, but Kevin, my assistant, will help you. We're open from 9 to 6 every day apart from Sundays. The overalls have also arrived, one in size M and one in size XL for £ 2.50 each.
Oh, and there's also a special offer on paint brushes next week. 25 % off all brushes and rollers. I think that might be interesting for you as well. Just call me on 4895414 if you have any further questions or come down to the shop whenever you like. Thank you.

New colour:	21	cream
New price:	22	£ 12
Shop assistant's name:	23	Kevin
Sizes of overalls:	24	M and XL
Special offer:	25	25 % off all brushes and rollers

Speaking

Part 2

CELINA (CANDIDATE B): Can you tell me where I can learn to **paint**?
JONAS (CANDIDATE A): Yes, you can go to the Swan's art school.
CELINA (CANDIDATE B): Do you know when the lessons are? (What time are the lessons?)
JONAS (CANDIDATE A): There are classes for teenagers every afternoon from 2 to 4.
CELINA (CANDIDATE B): Do you need to bring anything?
JONAS (CANDIDATE A): You must bring brushes and paper (and you should wear old clothes).
CELINA (CANDIDATE B): What about the price? (How much are the lessons?)
JONAS (CANDIDATE A): 10 lessons are 75 pounds. (The price is 75 pounds for ten lessons.)
CELINA (CANDIDATE B): Do you have a telephone number?
JONAS (CANDIDATE A): Yes, of course, it's 93 72 47. (Yes, of course. You can call 83 72 47 and start tomorrow.)
CELINA (CANDIDATE B): Thank you.
JONAS (CANDIDATE A): You're welcome.

JONAS (CANDIDATE A): Do you know more about **Mega Diggers**?
CELINA (CANDIDATE B): Yes, of course. What would you like to know?
JONAS (CANDIDATE A): Can you tell me what I can do there?
CELINA (CANDIDATE B): You can use all the equipment on the building site like diggers, caterpillars and so on.
JONAS (CANDIDATE A): Sounds good. How much do they charge? (And what does it cost?)
CELINA (CANDIDATE B): You pay 100 pounds per day.
JONAS (CANDIDATE A): Wow, that's a lot. What is included?
CELINA (CANDIDATE B): The price includes insurance and a buffet lunch.
JONAS (CANDIDATE A): OK, do you know about the opening hours?
CELINA (CANDIDATE B): Yes, the building site is open from Wednesday to Sunday between 10 am and 9 pm.
JONAS (CANDIDATE A): Are there any special arrangements?
CELINA (CANDIDATE B): Yes, there are events for schools, companies and families.
JONAS (CANDIDATE A): That sounds interesting. Thank you very much.
CELINA (CANDIDATE B): Not at all.

Sprachenzertifikat Englisch A2
Mock Exam 5

Paper 1: Reading and Writing

Part 1

Questions 1–5
*Which notice (**A–H**) says this (**1–5**)?*
*For questions 1–5, mark the correct letters **A–H** on your answer sheet.*

Example:

0. You get 50 % off the price this week. [C]

1. You can call someone if you need help. [ ]
2. This place opens at weekends only. [ ]
3. This is not open to everyone in the mornings. [ ]
4. You can buy coffee in different cups here. [ ]
5. To go there you must join a club first. [ ]

A skateboard lessons
3 afternoons a week

B Toy Museum open Sat/Sun
adults £ 2.00 – children £ 1.50

C SUMMER SALE
swimsuits at half price this week

D Teachers' car park
open to all from 2 pm

E Buy a mobile phone and get
a £ 15.00 phone card for free!

F Chess club - members only

G Hot drinks to go!
All drinks in sizes M – L – XL

H If you have problems operating the machine
phone Kevin on 85748367

Part 2

Questions 6–10
Read the sentences about spending time in a park.
*Choose the best word (**A, B** or **C**) for each space.*
*For questions 6–10, mark **A**, **B** or **C** on your answer sheet.*

Example:

0. For Ben and Josh the park is the … place to be in summer.

   A ☐ good **B** ☐ most **C** ☑ best

6. They … at the entrance after school whenever they can.

   A ☐ meeting **B** ☐ meets **C** ☐ meet

7. First they … their favourite animals.

   A ☐ look **B** ☐ visit **C** ☐ are looking forward

8. Josh … brings food and the boys have a picnic.

   A ☐ never **B** ☐ sometimes **C** ☐ many

9. They sit under the trees and … to some good music on Ben's CD player.

   A ☐ listening **B** ☐ hear **C** ☐ listen

10. When it is getting dark Josh and Ben … home on their bikes.

    A ☐ drive **B** ☐ travel **C** ☐ ride

Part 3

Questions 11–15
Complete the five conversations.
*For questions 11–15, mark **A**, **B** or **C** on your answer sheet.*

Example:

0. Did you understand what the teacher said?

   A ☐ Nothing special.
   B ☑ Not really.
   C ☐ It's not enough.

11. Would you like another drink?

    A ☐ No thanks, I'm fine.
    B ☐ No, not at all.
    C ☐ Yes, go ahead.

12. Do you like tennis?
- **A** ☐ Usually twice a week.
- **B** ☐ I prefer football.
- **C** ☐ I'm a very good player.

13. I think Peter is on holiday.
- **A** ☐ I love Spain.
- **B** ☐ When will he be back?
- **C** ☐ When does he arrive?

14. Do you also live in Brighton?
- **A** ☐ Yes, I come from England.
- **B** ☐ No, from Birmingham.
- **C** ☐ No, I'm from Dover.

15. Have a nice weekend.
- **A** ☐ Yes, please.
- **B** ☐ The same to you!
- **C** ☐ You're welcome.

Questions 16–20
Complete the conversation between two friends.
What does Bob say to Charlotte?
For questions 16–20, mark the correct letter ***A–H*** *on your answer sheet.*

Example:

Charlotte: Hello Bob. Nice to see you.

Bob: **0.** B

Charlotte: I'm going shopping. Would you like to come?

Bob: **16.** ______

Charlotte: Yes, I wanted to go there first because I need some tennis balls.

Bob: **17.** ______

Charlotte: OK, and then we could go to the café.

Bob **18.** ______

Charlotte: The one next to the sports shop. I'm meeting Sarah and Tom there at 4 pm.

Bob: **19.** ______

Charlotte: Why do you want to speak to him?

Bob: **20.** ______

Charlotte: That's true. He's helped me a lot, too.

A Oh, good. I need a new baseball cap.

B Nice to see you, too. What are you doing?

C Brilliant. I need to speak to Tom anyway.

D Yes, are you going to the sports shop?

E Which one?

F Tom is very nice indeed.

G The café is in Bond street.

H Well, because I don't understand our homework and Tom is very good at maths.

Part 4

Questions 21–27
Read the text about the Titanic and then answer the questions.
*For questions 21–27, mark **A**, **B** or **C** on your answer sheet.*

The Titanic

When the Titanic started from Southampton to New York on 10 April 1912 she was the biggest ship in the world. Many rich people had booked passages for the first voyage on the luxurious ship. But there were also a lot of poor people on board who wanted to find a better life in America. Everyone had heard that the Titanic was unsinkable because her bottom had been divided into sixteen watertight compartments. Four days after the Titanic had left Southampton she was sailing through a very cold but quiet night. Captain Smith went to bed and told First Officer Murdoch to watch out for icebergs. When lookout Fleet shouted at 23.40 "iceberg right ahead!" First Officer Murdoch still could not see it because the iceberg was very dark and grey. When he heard the noise, Captain Smith ran onto the bridge immediately. The passengers were not afraid at first. They were sure the Titanic would not sink. Captain Smith, however, knew that the situation was very dangerous. The crew was trying to get people into lifeboats, women and children first. But there were not enough boats for everyone and when the ship sank at 2.20 more than 1,500 people lost their lives.

Example:

0. The Titanic started in
   A ☐ America.
   B ☐ New York.
   C ☑ Southampton.

21. Some passengers
   A ☐ had lived in America all their lives.
   B ☐ were very rich.
   C ☐ wanted to start a new life in Southampton.

22. People believed the ship was
   A ☐ very safe.
   B ☐ sinkable.
   C ☐ not safe at all.

23. The disaster happened
   A ☐ near Southampton.
   B ☐ after four days at sea.
   C ☐ because the compartments were not watertight.

24. When the Titanic hit the iceberg
A ☐ the sea was very rough.
B ☐ it was very cold.
C ☐ it was a cloudy night.

25. First Officer Murdoch
A ☐ saw the iceberg immediately.
B ☐ thought the iceberg was not very big.
C ☐ could not see the iceberg at once.

26. Captain Smith
A ☐ had not told his First Officer about icebergs.
B ☐ was on the bridge when the Titanic hit the iceberg.
C ☐ ran onto the bridge when the ship had hit the iceberg.

27. When the Titanic sank at 2.20 am
A ☐ a huge number of people lost their lives.
B ☐ there were lifeboats for all passengers.
C ☐ the crew got in the lifeboats first.

Part 5

Questions 28–35
*Read the article. Choose the best answer (**A**, **B** or **C**) for each space.*
*For answers 28–35, mark **A**, **B** or **C** on your answer sheet.*

LONDON EYE

Among the many attractions for tourists, the London Eye is one of the (0) ___most___ modern. Constructed by Marks Barfield architects it opened for the public (28) __________ March 2000. On its first birthday 3.5 million people (29) __________ already visited it.

The big wheel turns at a speed (30) __________ about 0.9 kms per hour. This means it does not have to stop to (31) __________ passengers step into the capsules. (32) __________ of the egg shaped glass capsules is air-conditioned and (33) __________ carry a maximum of 25 people. (34) __________ a clear day you can see up to 40 kms from the top of the 135 m high wheel. One full rotation (35) __________ about 30 minutes.

Example:

	A		B		C	
0.	☐	best	☐	much	☑	most
28.	☐	from	☐	in	☐	by
29.	☐	have	☐	had	☐	will
30.	☐	from	☐	by	☐	of
31.	☐	letting	☐	lets	☐	let
32.	☐	Each	☐	Every	☐	All
33.	☐	could	☐	can	☐	take
34.	☐	On	☐	With	☐	At
35.	☐	take	☐	took	☐	takes

Part 6

Questions 36–40
Read the descriptions of some electrical appliances you can find at home.
What is the word for each one?
The first letter is already there. There is one space for each other letter in the word.
For questions 36–40, write the words on your answer sheet.

Example:

0. When it's getting dark you switch on the l i g h t.

36. When you want warm, crispy bread you put it in the t _ _ _ _ _ _.

37. When you've washed your hair you can use a h _ _ _ _ _ _ _ _.

38. People who work from home often use a computer or a l _ _ _ _ _.

39. You can listen to your favourite music on a C _ _ _ _ _ _ _.

40. When it is cold in winter you turn on the h _ _ _ _ _ _.

Part 7

Questions 41–50
Complete the emails. Write ***one*** *word for each space.*
For questions 41–50, write the words on your answer sheet.

Example: (0) *to*

Untitled - Message (Plain Text)

File Edit View Insert Format Tools Actions Help

Send | Accounts | Options...

To... fred.suttner@web.co.uk

Cc...

Bcc...

Subject: Tent/Lake District

Dear Mr Suttner,

I (**0**) ___*am*___ writing to you from the Lake District. We are staying (**41**) ____________ a very nice campsite here. We bought a new tent (**42**) ____________ your shop last week. When we arrived here we found that (**43**) ____________ parts were missing. We (**44**) ____________ not put up the tent and my parents (**45**) ____________ to rent another one.

Kind regards,

Penny Loy

Untitled - Message (Plain Text)

File Edit View Insert Format Tools Actions Help

Send | Accounts | Options...

To... penny.loy@loys.co.uk

Cc...

Bcc...

Subject: Tent/Lake District

Dear Penny,

Of course I (**46**) ____________ pay for the tent you rented. I spoke (**47**) ____________ the maker of the tent you bought. They are (**48**) ____________ to send a new one this week. You will also get a rucksack from them (**49**) ____________ you had so much trouble.

Give my regards to (**50**) ____________ parents.

Best wishes,

Fred Suttner

Part 8

Questions 51–55
Read the job advert and the letter.
Fill in the information on the form.
For questions 51–55, write the information on your answer sheet.

Dear Paul,

I saw this advert in our newspaper. It's the perfect summer job for you. They are looking for young people for a play at the castle. You'd be playing the audience, so you don't need experience. You'll get £ 22 per evening, more than the £ 20 you had in the garden centre last year! The working hours are ideal: 8.30 - 10 pm. There is going to be a training & information day on May 28. The play will start on July 2 and will be performed Wed., Fri., Sat. until August 3.

Auntie Helen

P.S. Call me on my new phone no. 956046 to let me know what you think.

Boys & Girls wanted for summer job

Must be 16 – 22 years
Full instruction given
3 evenings a week

Call Melissa on 934846 for details

Paul's notes:		
Date of training day:	**51**	____________
Money per evening:	**52**	£ ____________
Working hours:	**53**	____________
Helen's new phone no.:	**54**	____________
For further information speak to:	**55**	____________

Part 9

Question 56
Read the following email from your friend Ron:

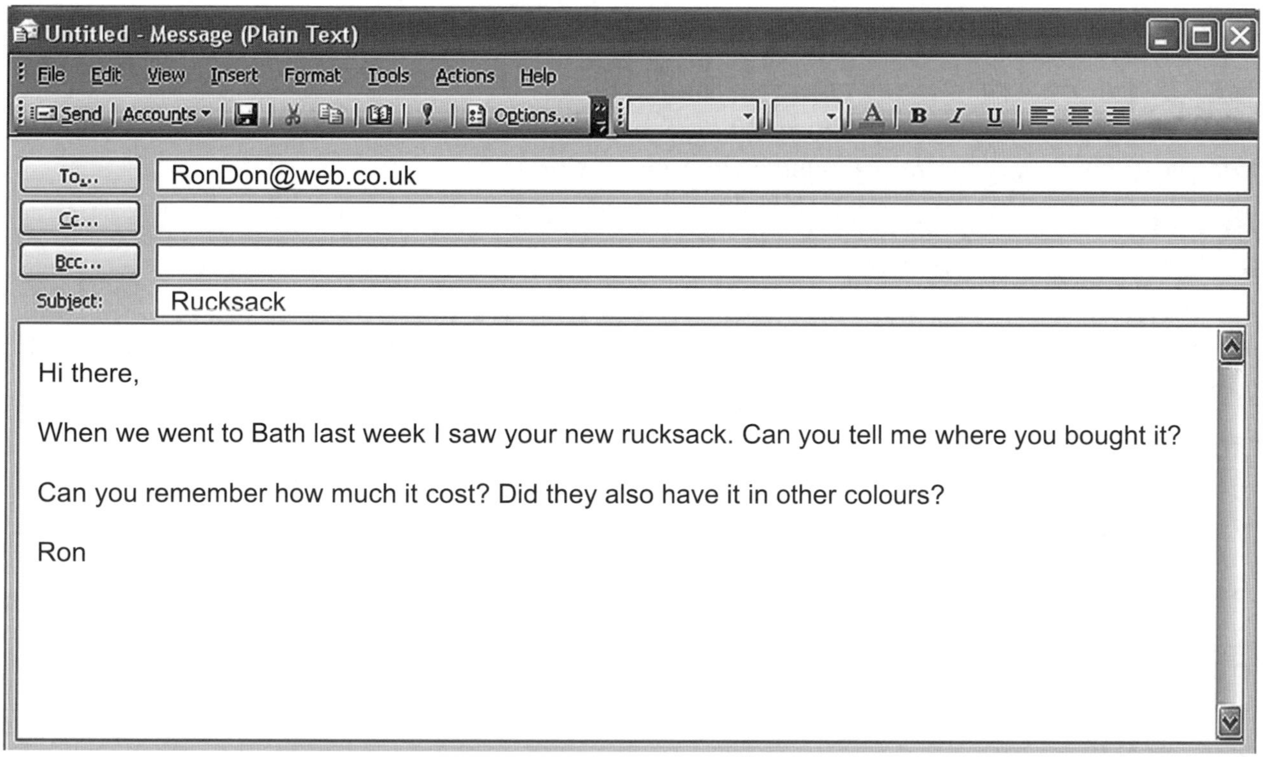
Untitled - Message (Plain Text)

File Edit View Insert Format Tools Actions Help

Send | Accounts | Options...

To...: RonDon@web.co.uk

Cc...:

Bcc...:

Subject: Rucksack

Hi there,

When we went to Bath last week I saw your new rucksack. Can you tell me where you bought it?

Can you remember how much it cost? Did they also have it in other colours?

Ron

Write an email to Ron and answer his questions.
Write 25–35 words.
Write on your answer sheet.

Paper 2: Listening

Part 1

Tracks 37–41

You will hear five short conversations.
You will hear each conversation twice.
There is one question for each conversation.
For questions 1–5, put a tick (✓) under the right answer.

Example:

0. When did the concert start?

WOMAN: Did the concert start at three o'clock yesterday?
MAN: No, they had planned to start at three thirty but the bus was late so they started at four.

A ☐

B ☐

C ☑

1. Which pizza does the man want?

A ☐

B ☐

C ☐

2. What is Emily wearing today?

A ☐

B ☐

C ☐

3. What happened to Neil last week?

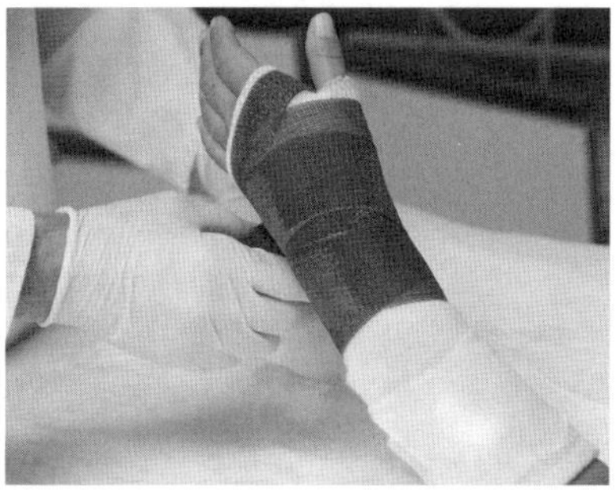

A ☐

B ☐

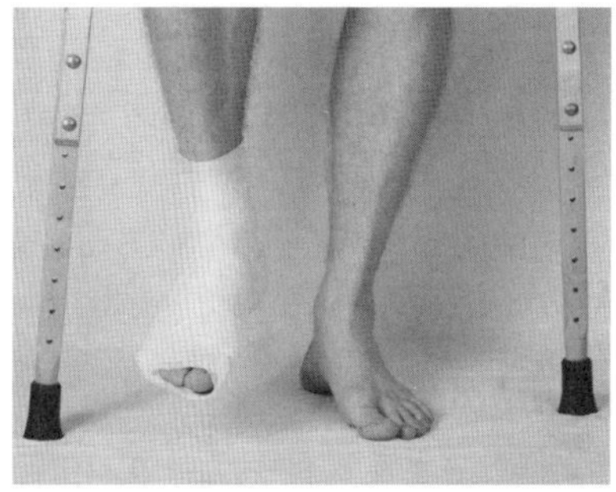

C ☐

4. Why didn't Holly come to the party?

A ☐

B ☐

C ☐

5. What did Alison buy?

A ☐

B ☐

C ☐

Part 2

Track 42

Questions 6–10
The music school has an open day next week. Who is doing what?
Listen and complete the list.
*For questions 6–10, write a letter (**A–H**) next to the people.*
You will hear the conversation twice.

Example:

0.	Paul	A	**A**	piano
6.	Laura	☐	**B**	drums
7.	Susan	☐	**C**	sing
8.	Peter	☐	**D**	trumpet
9.	Bob	☐	**E**	guitar
10.	Andy	☐	**F**	clarinet
			G	bass
			H	violin

Part 3

Track 43

Questions 11–15
Listen to Sam and Penny talking about a computer exhibition.
*For questions 11–15, tick (✓) **A**, **B** or **C**.*
You will hear the conversation twice.

Example:

0. When did Penny go to the exhibition?
   A ☐ Yesterday
   B ☑ The day before yesterday
   C ☐ Tuesday

11. What did Penny think of the presentation?
   A ☐ It was too long.
   B ☐ It was interesting.
   C ☐ It was boring.

12. Penny wants to become
   A ☐ a hairdresser.
   B ☐ a journalist.
   C ☐ a teacher.

13. What did they get from one software producer?
A ☐ A picture
B ☐ A manual
C ☐ A CD

14. Where is Softhair's stand?
A ☐ Hall B, left
B ☐ Main entrance, right
C ☐ Hall B, right

15. What did Penny buy at the exhibition?
A ☐ A book
B ☐ A bag
C ☐ A camcorder

Track 44

Part 4

Questions 16–20
You will hear a conversation about a house for rent.
Listen and complete questions 16–20.
You will hear the conversation twice.

House for rent		
Owner's name:		George Garrett
Number of bedrooms:	**16**	________________ (+ 1 room)
Minimum stay:	**17**	______________________________
Nearest shop:	**18**	____________________ 2 kms away
In the garden shed:	**19**	Bikes and a __________ for children
Distance to the beach:	**20**	____________________________ m

Part 5

Track 45

Questions 21–25
You will hear a recorded message.
Listen and complete questions 21–25.
You will hear the information twice.

Local Ticket Service Line		
Derby tickets left for section(s):	**21**	________________
For Sunday match must arrive at:	**22**	________ pm
Order tickets for outdoor theatre by fax or:	**23**	________________
Outdoor theatre:	**24**	£ ____________ price for adults
Midnight buffet now at:	**25**	________________

You now have 8 minutes to write your answers on the answer sheet.

Paper 3: Speaking

Part 1

Part 1 consists of a short conversation with the examiner. You should be familiar with the language associated with meeting people for the first time and you should be able to give information of a personal kind, e. g name, place of origin, occupation, family etc. You are also expected to talk about your daily life, your hobbies etc.

Part 2

Prompt cards are used to stimulate questions and answers. The examiner gives instructions and hands out a question card to one candidate and an answer card to the other. After the candidates have asked and answered their questions, they change roles.

Example

The examiner gives a question card to Candidate B and an answer card to Candidate A.

Candidate A, here is some information about a car show.

Candidate B, you don't know anything about this car show, so ask A some questions about it. Now B, ask A your questions about this car show and A, you answer them.

Candidate A – your information.

Car Show

Saturday 23 May ° 10 am – 7 pm ° Market square

See cars from last 100 years ° test drive new cars

Snacks and drinks sold

Candidate B – your questions.

Car Show

- When?
- What to see/do?
- Where?
- Food?
- Hours?

Candidate B, here is some information about this special honey.

Candidate A, you don't know anything about this special honey, so ask B some questions about it. Now A, ask B your questions about this special honey and B, you answer them.

Candidate B – your information.

Candidate A – your questions.

Special Honey

- Why special?
- Other products?
- Price?
- When open?
- Who?

Lösungsvorschläge

Reading and Writing

Part 1

1. You can call someone if you need help. **H**
2. This place opens at weekends only. **B**
3. This is not open to everyone in the mornings. **D**
4. You can buy coffee in different cups here. **G**
5. To go there you must join a club first. **F**

Part 2

6. They … at the entrance after school whenever they can.

   A ☐ meeting **B** ☐ meets **C** ☑ meet

7. First they … their favourite animals.

   A ☐ look **B** ☑ visit **C** ☐ are looking forward

8. Josh … brings food and the boys have a picnic.

   A ☐ never **B** ☑ sometimes **C** ☐ many

9. They sit under the trees and … to some good music on Ben's CD player.

   A ☐ listening **B** ☐ hear **C** ☑ listen

10. When it is getting dark Josh and Ben … home on their bikes.

    A ☐ drive **B** ☐ travel **C** ☑ ride

Part 3

11. Would you like another drink?
- **A** ☑ No thanks, I'm fine.
- **B** ☐ No, not at all.
- **C** ☐ Yes, go ahead.

12. Do you like tennis?
- **A** ☐ Usually twice a week.
- **B** ☑ I prefer football.
- **C** ☐ I'm a very good player.

13. I think Peter is on holiday.
- **A** ☐ I love Spain.
- **B** ☑ When will he be back?
- **C** ☐ When does he arrive?

14. Do you also live in Brighton?
- **A** ☐ Yes, I come from England.
- **B** ☐ No, from Birmingham.
- **C** ☑ No, I'm from Dover.

15. Have a nice weekend.
- **A** ☐ Yes, please.
- **B** ☑ The same to you!
- **C** ☐ You're welcome.

Charlotte: I'm going shopping. Would you like to come?

Bob: **16.** D

Charlotte: Yes, I wanted to go there first because I need some tennis balls.

Bob: **17.** A

Charlotte: OK, and then we could go to the café.

Bob **18.** E

Charlotte: The one next to the sports shop. I'm meeting Sarah and Tom there at 4 pm.

Bob: **19.** C

Charlotte: Why do you want to speak to him?

Bob: **20.** H

Charlotte: That's true. He's helped me a lot, too.

Part 4

21. Some passengers
- A ☐ had lived in America all their lives.
- B ☑ were very rich.
- C ☐ wanted to start a new life in Southampton.

22. People believed the ship was
- A ☑ very safe.
- B ☐ sinkable.
- C ☐ not safe at all.

23. The disaster happened
- A ☐ near Southampton.
- B ☑ after four days at sea.
- C ☐ because the compartments were not watertight.

24. When the Titanic hit the iceberg
- A ☐ the sea was very rough.
- B ☑ it was very cold.
- C ☐ it was a cloudy night.

25. First Officer Murdoch
- A ☐ saw the iceberg immediately.
- B ☐ thought the iceberg was not very big.
- C ☑ could not see the iceberg at once.

26. Captain Smith
- A ☐ had not told his First Officer about icebergs.
- B ☐ was on the bridge when the Titanic hit the iceberg.
- C ☑ ran onto the bridge when the ship had hit the iceberg.

27. When the Titanic sank at 2.20 am
- A ☑ a huge number of people lost their lives.
- B ☐ there were lifeboats for all passengers.
- C ☐ the crew got in the lifeboats first.

Part 5

	A	B	C
28.	☐ from	☑ in	☐ by
29.	☐ have	☑ had	☐ will
30.	☐ from	☐ by	☑ of
31.	☐ letting	☐ lets	☑ let
32.	☑ Each	☐ Every	☐ All

33.	**A**	☐ could	**B**	☑ can	**C**	☐ take
34.	**A**	☑ On	**B**	☐ With	**C**	☐ At
35.	**A**	☐ take	**B**	☐ took	**C**	☑ takes

Part 6

36. When you want warm, crispy bread you put it in the **toaster**.

37. When you've washed your hair you can use a **hairdryer**.

38. People who work from home often use a computer or a **laptop**.

39. You can listen to your favourite music on a **CD player**.

40. When it is cold in winter you turn on the **heating**.

Part 7

Dear Mr Suttner,
I **am** writing to you from the Lake District.We are staying **(41)** **at** a very nice campsite here. We bought a new tent **(42)** **from/at/in** your shop last week. When we arrived here we found that **(43)** **some/several/a few** parts were missing. We **(44)** **could** not put up the tent and my parents **(45)** **had** to rent another one.

Kind regards,
Penny Loy

Dear Penny,
Of course I **(46)** **will** pay for the tent you rented. I spoke **(47)** **to/with** the maker of the tent you bought. They are **(48)** **going** to send a new one this week. You will also get a rucksack from them **(49)** **because** you had so much trouble. Give my regards to **(50)** **your** parents.

Best wishes,
Fred Suttner

Part 8

Date of training day:	51	May 28
Money per evening:	52	£ 22
Working hours:	53	8.30 - 10 pm
Helen's new phone no.:	54	956046
For further information speak to:	55	Melissa

Part 9

Hi Ron,
I bought the rucksack from "Sports Corner" in the shopping centre. It was £ 19.00, but I think it was a special offer. They also had it in red and blue.
See you soon,

Es müssen alle **drei Punkte** behandelt werden. Das Schreiben **muss mindestens 25 Worte** lang sein.

Listening

Part 1

Tracks 37–41

1. **Which pizza does the man want?**
   WOMAN: I'll have cheese and onion.
   MAN: I think I'll take tomato. Or no, ham and cheese is better.
   WOMAN: In the end you always have ham and cheese.

2. **What is Emily wearing today?**
   MAN: Is that Emily over there in the dark trousers?
   WOMAN: No, she's wearing a skirt today.
   MAN: Oh, yes, now I can see her. Look, she's also wearing her new hat.

3. **What happened to Neil last week?**
   WOMAN: Neil broke his arm last week.
   MAN: Oh, no. He's very unlucky. Last year he broke his leg.
   WOMAN: Yes, I know. And his bike was stolen last summer, too.

4. **Why didn't Holly come to the party?**
   MAN: Why didn't you come to the party last night?
   WOMAN: I wanted to, but first I did some shopping. And when I got home my boss had mailed me a report to finish. That's why I couldn't go out in the evening.
   MAN: What a pity, it was a good party. Anyway, would you like to go to the cinema on Friday?

5. **What did Alison buy?**
   BOY: What did you buy from the baker's?
   GIRL: A loaf of bread and two muffins.
   BOY: Didn't you bring the milk for Henry?
   GIRL: Oh, yes of course. I got that as well.

1. Which pizza does the man want?

A ☐

B ☐

C ☑

2. What is Emily wearing today?

A ☐

B ☐

C ☑

3. What happened to Neil last week?

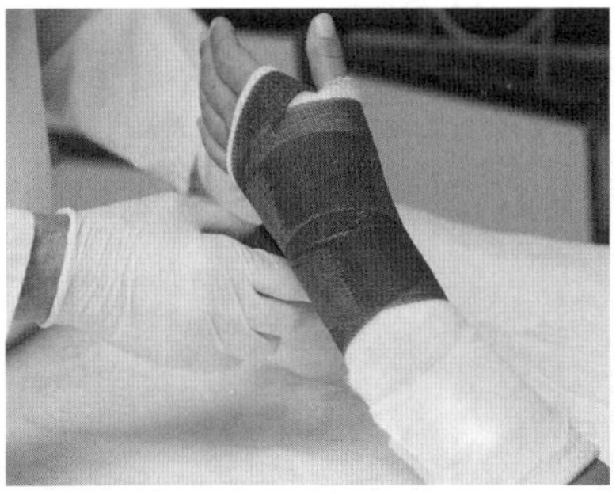

A ☑

B ☐

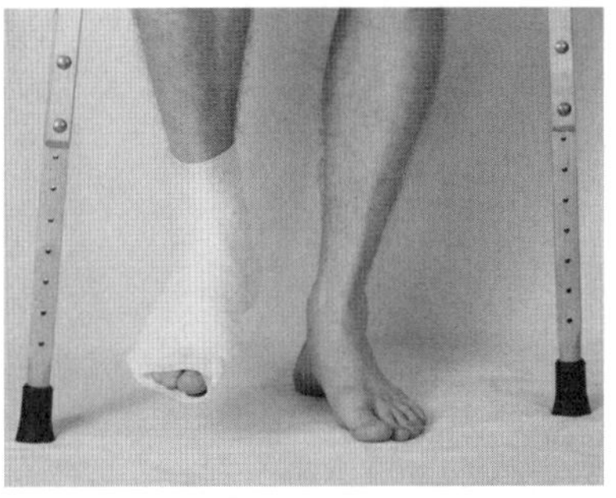

C ☐

4. Why didn't Holly come to the party?

A ☐

B ☑

C ☐

5. What did Alison buy?

A ☐

B ☑

C ☐

Part 2

Track 42

Girl: So who is doing what at the music school open day next week? Paul, I think you're playing the piano, aren't you?

Boy: Yes, that's right. And Laura's going to sing?

Girl: Actually, Sarah wanted to sing but she's got a cold, so now Laura is singing.

Boy: What about the trumpet players?

Girl: On my list it says Bob or Andy is going to play the trumpet.

Boy: Let's take Bob. He's not here today but he's very good.

Girl: Is anyone here who'd like to play the guitar? Susan, what about you?

Other girl: OK, but I thought I should play the violin.

Boy: No, Peter's doing that now. He's been practising all week.

Girl: Typical. He's also a very good clarinet player.

Boy: Yes, he is. So all we need now is a bass player. How about you, Andy?

Other Boy: Alright, if you don't want me to sing.

Laughter

6. Laura **C**
7. Susan **E**
8. Peter **H**
9. Bob **D**
10. Andy **G**

Part 3

Track 43

Sam: Hi Penny. Did you visit the computer exhibition yesterday?

Penny: Hello Sam. No, in fact we went the day before yesterday.

Sam: We're going on Tuesday. I'm so excited. You must tell me everything.

Penny: Well, when we arrived there was a presentation by MegaTec. I found it a bit boring, but it didn't take long.

Sam: And then, what was next?

Penny: We saw some new text editing software. That was really good, I thought. I want to become a journalist, you see. My dad wants me to be a teacher, though.

Sam: Didn't they have anything funny?

Penny: Oh, yes, they did. Do you know the software where you can try hairstyles? They showed us the manual and we played with it for an hour. In the end we all got a picture from the company showing us with funny hairstyles.

Sam: I've got to tell Peter and Ken – we have to go there. Where's their stand?

Penny: They're called Softhair and the stand is in hall B on the right-hand side. You can't miss it. It's just opposite the main entrance.

Sam: Did they have the new camcorders, too?

PENNY: Oh, yes, we tried all the new models. They're really easy to use and the quality's fantastic.
SAM: Did you buy anything?
PENNY: Well, I wanted to buy a camcorder but then I couldn't decide. So I just bought a new bag for my laptop.

11. What did Penny think of the presentation?
 A ☐ It was too long.
 B ☐ It was interesting.
 C ☑ It was boring.

12. Penny wants to become
 A ☐ a hairdresser.
 B ☑ a journalist.
 C ☐ a teacher.

13. What did they get from one software producer?
 A ☑ A picture
 B ☐ A manual
 C ☐ A CD

14. Where is Softhair's stand?
 A ☐ Hall B, left
 B ☐ Main entrance, right
 C ☑ Hall B, right

15. What did Penny buy at the exhibition?
 A ☐ A book
 B ☑ A bag
 C ☐ A camcorder

Part 4

Track 44

MAN: Good morning. This is George Garrett speaking.
WOMAN: Good morning, I'd like some information about the house you rent out at the beach.
MAN: Oh yes, of course. Did you see our advert in the paper?
WOMAN: Yes, I did. We're a big family so we need a house with at least 3 bedrooms.
MAN: Well, the house has 4 bedrooms and another room with a big sofa.
WOMAN: Great. We'd like to go in July. Is the house free then?
MAN: Yes, no problem. But you'll have to stay for at least a week.
WOMAN: We wanted two weeks anyway, so that's fine. Can you tell me a bit more about the area?
MAN: Yes, er … there's a swimming pool and the nearest supermarket is 2 kms away. You'll find a shopping centre in the village, about 7 kms away.
WOMAN: Sounds very good.
MAN: And there's a large garden with a barbecue area. In the shed there're bikes and a boat for the children.

WOMAN: How far is it to the beach?
MAN: Only about 500 metres. You have a nice sea view from the balcony. And there's a little café on the beach, only 700 metres away.
WOMAN: OK, thank you very much. I'll send you an email with our details.
MAN: OK, thank you. Goodbye.
WOMAN: Goodbye.

Number of bedrooms:	**16**	4 (+ 1 room)
Minimum stay:	**17**	1/a week
Nearest shop:	**18**	supermarket 2 kms away
In the garden shed:	**19**	Bikes and a boat for children
Distance to the beach:	**20**	500 m

Part 5

Track 45

Hello. You have called the local ticket service line. You will now hear which tickets are still available for the coming weekend.
For the football derby on Saturday we only have tickets left for section C. For the Sunday match at 3 pm there are tickets for sections A, C and D. Please note that you must be at the football stadium at 2.30 at the latest.
Tickets for the outdoor theatre must be ordered by fax or email. They cost £15 for adults and £7.50 for children up to 12. There is one evening performance on May 22 at 8 pm. You must arrive at 7.30 at the latest. The midnight buffet will be at the theatre and not at the town hall, as printed in some newspapers. There is a seat plan for all plays on our webpage, where you can see exactly which seats are still free.
If you need further information, please press 4 and we will connect you to one of our employees.

Derby tickets left for section(s):	21	C
For Sunday match must arrive at:	22	2.30 pm
Order tickets for outdoor theatre by fax or:	23	email
Outdoor theatre:	24	Price for adults: £ 15
Midnight buffet now at:	25	theatre

Speaking

Part 2

LUCAS (CANDIDATE B): Can you give me some details about the **car show**?
MELANIE (CANDIDATE A): Yes, what do you need to know?
LUCAS (CANDIDATE B): First of all do you know when the car show is on?
MELANIE (CANDIDATE A): On Saturday, the twenty-third of May. (It's on May twenty-third, a Saturday.)
LUCAS (CANDIDATE B): And what can you see and do there?
MELANIE (CANDIDATE A): Well, you can see cars from the last 100 years and also test-drive new cars.
LUCAS (CANDIDATE B): Where is the car show?
MELANIE (CANDIDATE A): It's on Market Square.
LUCAS (CANDIDATE B): Can you also get food there?
MELANIE (CANDIDATE A): Yes, you can get snacks and drinks.
LUCAS (CANDIDATE B): And do you know the opening hours?
MELANIE (CANDIDATE A): Let me see. Yes, it takes place from 10 am to 7 pm.
LUCAS (CANDIDATE B): OK, thank you very much then.
MELANIE (CANDIDATE A): You're very welcome.

MELANIE (CANDIDATE A): I need some information about this **special honey**. Can you help me, please?
LUCAS (CANDIDATE B): Let's see. What would you like to know?
MELANIE (CANDIDATE A): Why is this honey special? (What is so special about this honey?)
LUCAS (CANDIDATE B): It's top quality from local bees. (It's made by bees from this area and very good quality.)
MELANIE (CANDIDATE A): Do they sell other products as well?

LUCAS (CANDIDATE B): Yes, you can buy candles and sweets.
MELANIE (CANDIDATE A): Sounds good. How much is the honey? (What does the honey cost?)
LUCAS (CANDIDATE B): The honey is 3 pounds per glass.
MELANIE (CANDIDATE A): When is the shop open? (What are the shop's opening hours?)
LUCAS (CANDIDATE B): It's open from Wednesday to Friday between 2 and 5. (It's open from 2 to 5 in the afternoon from Wednesday to Friday.)
MELANIE (CANDIDATE A): Who do I need to speak to? (Who do I ask?/Who is the person in charge?)
LUCAS (CANDIDATE B): (The flyer says) ask for George.
MELANIE (CANDIDATE A): I will. Thank you very much.
LUCAS (CANDIDATE B): You're welcome.

Ideal zum selbstständigen Lernen in der 7. bis 10. Klasse

Englisch Training

- Schülergerecht aufbereiteter Lernstoff mit anschaulichen Beispielen, abwechslungsreichen Übungen und erklärende Lösungen zum selbstständigen Lernen zu Hause.
- Schließt Wissenslücken und gibt Sicherheit und Motivation durch Erfolgserlebnisse.

Grundwissen Hauptschule

Englisch Grundwissen 9. Klasse .... Best.-Nr. 93451
Englisch Hörverstehen 9. Klasse mit CD ... Best.-Nr. 93452

Grundwissen Realschule

Englisch Grundwissen
7. Klasse Realschule .... Best.-Nr. 914510
Englisch Grundwissen 8. Klasse .... Best.-Nr. 90508
Englisch Grundwissen 9. Klasse .... Best.-Nr. 90509
Englisch Grundwissen 10. Klasse .... Best.-Nr. 90510
Englisch Grundwissen
Übertritt in die Oberstufe........................ Best.-Nr. 82453
Textproduktion 9./10. Klasse................. Best.-Nr. 90541
Hörverstehen 10. Klasse mit CD .... Best.-Nr. 91457
Systematische Vokabelsammlung .... Best.-Nr. 91455

Grundwissen Gymnasium

Englisch Grundwissen 8. Klasse (G8)....... Best.-Nr. 90508
Englisch Grundwissen 9. Klasse (G8)....... Best.-Nr. 90509
Englisch Grundwissen 10. Klasse (G8)..... Best.-Nr. 90510
Englisch Grundwissen
Übertritt in die Oberstufe (G8) .... Best.-Nr. 82453
Textproduktion 9./10. Klasse (G8) .... Best.-Nr. 90541
Hörverstehen 10. Klasse mit CD (G8) ..... Best.-Nr. 80457
Leseverstehen 8. Klasse (G8)................. Best.-Nr. 90522
Leseverstehen 10. Klasse (G8)............... Best.-Nr. 90521
Wortschatzübung Mittelstufe (G8).......... Best.-Nr. 90520
Englische Rechtschreibung
9./10. Klasse (G8)................................ Best.-Nr. 80453

Ratgeber für Schüler

Die Ratgeber bieten wertvolle Tipps und Tricks für dauerhaften Lernerfolg.

Richtig Lernen – Tipps und Lernstrategien
7. – 10. Klasse .... Best.-Nr. 10482

Englisch Kompakt-Wissen

Prüfungsrelevantes Wissen in Kompaktform – die prägnante Gedächtnisstütze. Im praktischen Taschenbuchformat.

Englisch Themenwortschatz Hauptschule Best.-Nr. 934501
Englisch Grundwortschatz Hauptschule .. Best.-Nr. 934502
Englisch Themenwortschatz Realschule .. Best.-Nr. 914501
Englisch Grundwortschatz .... Best.-Nr. 90464
Englisch Kurzgrammatik .... Best.-Nr. 90461

Englisch Lektüre

Stark-Lektüren sind sprachlich den Kenntnissen der jeweiligen Klassenstufe angepasst. Mit Worterklärungen in deutscher Sprache.

Liam Cleary: Echoes and Other Short Stories
7. – 10. Klasse .... Best.-Nr. 250008
Rainer Jacob: Abenteuergeschichten 1
7. – 10. Klasse .... Best.-Nr. 80454

(Bitte blättern Sie um)